James B. Logan

# History of the Cumberland Presbyterian Church in Illinois

Containing sketches of the first ministers, churches, Presbyteries and Synods; also a history of missions, publication and education

James B. Logan

**History of the Cumberland Presbyterian Church in Illinois**
*Containing sketches of the first ministers, churches, Presbyteries and Synods; also a history of missions, publication and education*

ISBN/EAN: 9783337097172

Printed in Europe, USA, Canada, Australia, Japan

Cover: Foto ©Lupo / pixelio.de

More available books at **www.hansebooks.com**

# HISTORY

OF THE

# Cumberland Presbyterian Church

## IN ILLINOIS,

CONTAINING

*Sketches of the First Ministers, Churches, Presbyteries and Synods; also a History of Missions, Publication and Education.*

———◆———

By J. B. LOGAN, D.D.,

Author of "Alice McDonald," "Carrie Holmes," "Tract on Baptism," &c.

ALTON, ILL.:
Perrin & Smith, Book and Job Printers and Newspaper Publishers, State Street opposite Third.
1878.

TO ALL MINISTERS
OF THE
CUMBERLAND PRESBYTERIAN CHURCH IN ILLINOIS,
*Who have labored and sacrificed for
their love of her,*
THIS VOLUME IS FRATERNALLY DEDICATED.

# EXPLANATORY.

DEATH knocks with certain footsteps alike at the palace of the rich and the hut of the poor; at the counting-room of the merchant and the study of the man of God. His knock is imperative; and the rich and the poor, the merchant and the man of God, must as certainly answer. On the 14th of September, 1878, the Editor of this History threw down the gauntlet and gave up life's struggle. The course for him then ended; the race for him was run. Sad as every visitation of the dark messenger is, it is infinitely more so when a useful man is stricken down in his usefulness.

On account of the unexpected death of the Editor, the foregoing volume is imperfect in some respects. Just what his intention was in reference to this work is not fully known; but it has been carried out so far as ascertained. He evidently intended to prepare a full statistical table for the entire State, showing the numerical and financial strength of the denomination. Other matters of great interest he may have also intended to include in the volume. But he has gone, and there is no means of discovering the intended scope of the work. What is published is just as he left it, with no material alterations. The work is sent out with the hope that it may strengthen the bonds of the Church of God, re-animate and stimulate it, and glorify Him whose humble messenger the Editor was. May the blessings of Heaven go with it!

PUBLISHERS.

# CONTENTS.

Preface, 5
Introduction, 8

### CHAPTER I.
First Preachers, First Congregation, First Camp-Meeting, etc., 13

### CHAPTER II.
First Presbytery—When, Where, and by Whom Organized; Its Subsequent History for Several Years, 26

### CHAPTER III.
Sangamon Presbytery, 45

### CHAPTER IV.
The Third Presbytery—Vandalia, 52

### CHAPTER V.
Organization of the First Synod, 67

### CHAPTER VI.
Sangamon Synod, 72

### CHAPTER VII.
Central Illinois Synod, 83

### CHAPTER VIII.
Sketches of Some of the Oldest Churches in the State, 86

### CHAPTER IX.
Letters from Various Brethren in Reference to the Early Times of the Church in Illinois, 96

### CHAPTER X.
Missions and Publication, 109

### CHAPTER XI.
Educational Efforts, 121

### CHAPTER XII.
Mothers in Israel—Old Mother Barnes, Mrs. Ann Foster, and Mrs. Mary Ann Wilson, 132

### CHAPTER XIII.
Biographical—Revs. John Barber, Sen., D. W. McLin, J. M. Berry, A. W. Lansden, Joel Knight, Samuel McAdow, James Ashmore and William Finley, 140

### CHAPTER XIV.
Biographical, continued—Revs. Gilbert Dodds, David Foster, W. M. Hamilton, J. R. Lowrance, Cyrus Haynes, John Barber, Jr., Isaac Hill, John M. Cameron, Thomas Campbell, Nicholas Carper, and James McDowell, 181

# PREFACE.

THE origin and progress of the Cumberland Presbyterian Church has been not unlike a poor man who settles in the dense forest, a vast wilderness all around him. He first moves in on "government land," fells the trees, clears the ground of brush, builds his "log cabin," and gets in his little patch of corn. But all is on government soil—not a foot of the land is his. But through the forbearance of government he remains, and adds a little to his farm and flocks yearly. By slow and patient labor he gathers together finally enough money to "enter" his home at "a dollar and a quarter per acre." And it is a great day with him when he comes home to his family with a certificate from the land office for "a quarter section" of land. But watch him now a few years and you see the "little patch" of corn gives way to the large and broad farm; the "log cabin" has a large two-story frame or brick in front, with plenty of "out houses," and his flocks and herds fill large pastures. Prosperity smiles everywhere, and he begins to be regarded as one among the foremost farmers of his county. To look back forty years ago, it would seem impossible for him to have ever gained this high position.

So with the Cumberland Presbyterian Church. Never in the history of Christian churches did a denomination begin house-keeping with less facilities for the work, and darker prospects of success, than our fathers. We are aware that we have among us some who seem to see even yet nothing in the work and progress of our Church encouraging. We are not of the number. Every time we make a review, we leave off with a deeper impression and higher estimation of the marvelous work and sacrifices of our early fathers and people. That they succeeded at all, that they did not within the first ten years yield to surrounding embarrassments and give up all hope of perpetuating their organization, is to be accounted for simply and only that *the hand of God was in the movement.* It was never intended to be given up. And if Cumberland Presbyterians should betray their trust, and God in his anger should forsake us, rest assured the *principles* which originated and have thus far perpetuated this Church, will be crystalized in some form and be perpetuated by some organization to the end of time. At the birth of this Church the Protestant world was divided and arrayed into two antagonistic parties—Calvinists and Arminians. Each party was strong in numbers and wealth, and hoary with age. Each party agreed that if *their* side was not right that the other side must be, and therefore demanded that all men should receive one or the other theory as necessarily the truth. Cumberland Presbyterians were the first people on earth whose history is on record who undertook to plant their feet on "middle ground," and shun the extremes of both these systems. Of course they were ridiculed and laughed at, and treated like the builders of Jerusalem under Nehemiah. "What do these feeble Jews?" "Even that which they build if a fox go up it shall even break down their stone wall."—Neh. iv. 2, 3. But without prestige, or institutions of learning, books, papers, wealth, numbers, or fame to lean upon—like the woman with the ointment they have done what they could—and to-day we find both these great parties modifying gradually their *preaching*, if not their systems of divinity—until we find no scarcity of endorsers among all the Calvinistic and Arminian bodies of the peculiar doctrines of Cumberland Presbyterians, while sixty-eight years have worked a wonderful change in the Cumberland Presbyterian Church itself. This period has given us strong colleges, and, therefore, men in the front ranks of educated society. We are also beginning to have a literature not to be despised. From working at first in private houses and country school houses, we have gradually but surely found a permanent footing in some three or four hundred villages, towns and cities in the Mississippi Valley.

Beginning with church property of less than ten thousand dollars—all told—we have, according to the last statistics, $1,683,730, with twenty-one Presbyteries not reporting—the property of which will swell these figures to tens of thousands more. Nor does this estimate include our *college* property, which, if added, would make the figures at least $2,000,000. This is small compared with larger, older and much richer bodies; but from almost nothing sixty-eight years ago, it is not to be despised. Our membership is put down at 100,812, with ten Presbyteries reported at the figures of former years, and others defective. One hundred and twenty-five thousand communicants is not an extravagant estimate. And the amount contributed to Christ's cause in the past year is put down at $301,589, with thirty Presbyteries not reporting this item. The denomination has 458 probationers for the ministry, 1,283 ministers, 2,251 congregations. Well may we say, "What has God wrought?" With these facts before us, and the additional truth admitted by nearly all, that on those points of doctrine and practice which, at first, made the Cumberland Presbyterian Church distinctive, the theological changes of the last decade have invariably been a convergence toward these points, surely we have sufficient to stimulate to increased efforts and to satisfy us with our present and prospective position among the denominations of the great Protestant Church. Yet nothing would be more fatal than to rest here on our supposed laurels. We should only be inspired to greater faith, humility, zeal and consecration to the great work of the salvation of the race. While we "strengthen the stakes," we should "lengthen the cords" also. There is no success—there can be none without constant, persistent effort, and unreserved trust in God and his truth. While Paul "thanked God and took courage," it was not to sit down supinely, but his great soul was nerved for more vigorous labor,—so may the mercies of God to us only inspire us with stronger confidence in the truth, and greater zeal in its promulgation.

# INTRODUCTION.

I AM not insensible to the magnitude and delicacy of the task I have undertaken. It is one, however, which I have considered of great importance to the cause of Christ, and to Cumberland Presbyterians in particular. A true history of the Church is but a record of God's providences and dealings with men, in the kingdom of His grace. Not an unimportant portion of these special dealings and providences has God communicated to the world through the medium of the Cumberland Presbyterian Church. I know of no branch of the Church, for the time it has existed, which has been attended with greater marks of approbation from the great Head and King of Zion, than has been vouchsafed to us as a people. Wonderful seasons of refreshing and salvation, scarcely excelled by the day of Pentecost, attended the early ministrations of our fathers, and with some modifications, have continued with their sons in the ministry to the present time. At a very early day after the organization of the denomination in Dixon county, Tennessee, February 4, 1810, our ministers visited Illinois and planted the germ of the present Church on the soil of the great "Prairie State." This germ, though small and struggling for life for many years, has, with God's blessing, acquired finally a name and position among the permanent institutions of the country. Beginning here, as everywhere, poor in all things commonly regarded by the world as essential to success, yet a degree of prosperity has been attained by their labors not to be despised, even by those to whom greater facilities have been available.

## ORGANIZATION OF THE STATE.

Illinois was constituted a State in 1818, December 3. At that time the whole population of the State amounted to only a little over 35,000 persons. And yet, three years before this period, Cumberland Presbyterians had entered the territory and carried the glad tidings of salvation to its scattered inhabitants. Among the earliest ministrations the people of the State had from any source, were those from ministers of this then infant Church. And had it not been for the scarcity of ministers, the vast field to be cultivated, the want of ministerial support, and the poverty of the Church, in all human probability the Cumberland Presbyterian Church would have been to-day one of the leading denominations in this great State, if not entirely in *the* lead.

For long years she struggled against fearful difficulties. The Mother Church strongly opposed her efforts. Thousands found Christ under her ministrations and united with other sects, because they saw no prospect of permanency to our branch of Zion. Many meetings were held and souls converted where no opportunity was given to join our Church, because those holding the meetings did not expect to be there again and they had no prospect of a supply for the new members should they be willing to unite with them. The writer has held such meetings himself, and knows whereof he writes. Then the population for twenty or thirty years was more fluctuating, perhaps, than in any other of the new States or territories. A congregation might be organized this year, and two-thirds of its members gone before another year. The country was also regarded as uncommonly sickly, and although its rich soil was exceedingly inviting, yet but few, after shaking with ague, and burning with fever for months at a time, would not be anxious to get away where health could be enjoyed, even if other blessings were denied.

Another drawback to our Church in Illinois arose from the slavery question. The denomination originated in a slave

State, and although this question had nothing whatever to do in causing the Cumberland Presbyterian Church to be organized, nor was it mooted in the Confession of Faith, nor was the Church ever, in any proper sense, a *pro-slavery* church; yet many of our early ministers and members were necessarily connected with the institution, and Illinois being a free State, after the question came to be agitated, the emigration from the older parts of the Church flowed more freely into Missouri, Arkansas and Texas than into Illinois, for the obvious reason that any one holding slaves could carry them to any of the States named, but could not bring them to this State. However, such has been the success of Cumberland Presbyterians in this State that we feel justified in placing on permanent record such incidents of their history as are within reach, and as, we trust, will honor the Master and be useful to future generations.

We regret exceedingly that the task has not been undertaken by an abler pen, and before so many of the incidents of our early operations in the State had passed from memory. The most of the older brethren have passed away from earth, and nearly all of the remainder are removed to some other countries. For these reasons our history, especially of the early days of the Church, must necessarily be defective. Still, we feel like doing our best with the material within reach; and we are the more anxious to do this, when we remember that Illinois contains the ashes of one of that immortal trio who composed the first Presbytery, and who had the independence and the resolution to stand out before the world, even though it was at the expense of ecclesiastical ostracism, and declare that *truth* was better than worldly honor, that the approval of God was more to be coveted than the applause of men. We refer to Rev. Samuel McAdow, whose remains lie sleeping in the church-yard at old Mount Gilead, in Bond county. Scarcely less important is the fact that Rev. David Foster, also connected with the first Presbytery held, lived for years in Illinois, and whose remains are resting in Madison county. He was one of the immortal five licensed preachers, who was present at the organization of the Church in 1810, and who had been dealt with so summarily by the commission of Kentucky Synod. We never read the history of that event without feeling proud of those five young men who had the moral backbone to resist such an unwarrantable intrusion upon their rights. He spent several years of the latter part of his life in planting and watering the early churches in Illinois. A more detailed notice of these godly men will be found in the body of the work. David W. McLin, who was a candidate before the old Cumberland Presbytery, and who was an attendant at the first meeting of the new Cumberland Presbytery in March, 1810, was likewise a very successful minister in an early period in this State. Many, many will rise up in the great day and call him blessed. His labors were numerous and unceasing until death called him home. He, too, lies sleeping in the soil of Illinois.

Seeing, then, we have in the providence of God, the watch care over the dust of three of the *fathers* of the Church, who spent the prime of their days preaching Christ and establishing churches in this country, we feel we would be greatly recreant to our trust not to place in a permanent form something of the trials, labors, sufferings and successes of these men and their co-workers in this part of the Master's vineyard.

In the pages that follow, we are indebted for many items of history, and many interesting incidents, to a large number of brethren whose names it would be too tedious to mention. We may allude to the help derived from the "Biographical Sketches" by Dr. Beard, Dr. Crisman's "Origin and Doctrines," from the sketch of the life of Rev. Joel Knight in *Our Faith*, from other sketches from him in the *Cumberland Presbyterian;* but to none are we indebted more than to that old patriarch in the Church, Rev. Neill Johnson, of McMinnville, Oregon. He has taken a deep interest in our work from the start, and has rendered us invaluable service. His long and active life in the early days of the Church in Illinois, made him familiar with all the men and measures of the Church for many of the early years of its history. We shall let him speak largely in his own language in the proper place.

# CHAPTER I.

### FIRST PREACHERS—FIRST CONGREGATION—FIRST CAMP-MEETING, ETC.

ALL who have ever attempted any thing in the historical line, know how difficult it is to get at precise dates for any event which has transpired half a century ago, unless the dates were penned at the time the events transpired and have been preserved. We have found it exceedingly difficult to get satisfactory data about the first Cumberland Presbyterian minister who preached in the State—where and when he preached. Also equally difficult to be sure that we have found the organization of the first Cumberland Presbyterian congregation, and at what time and place. We have determined, however, to let the brethren whose recollection seems to differ about the matter speak for themselves, believing that this, upon the whole, will be more satisfactory to the reader. It will be seen from these papers that it was only four or five years at most from the time of the organization of the first Presbytery (Cumberland) in Tennessee, till some of these "Cumberlands" visited the Territory of Illinois, and preached Christ and a free and full salvation to the people. It will be seen that Rev. John Crawford, himself a pioneer, gives the honor of preaching the *first sermon* in the Territory of Illinois to Rev. John Barnett, in the year 1815, near Golconda; and that the first Cumberland Presbyterian family that ever crossed the Ohio River to reside in Illinois was the Tagert family, in 1813. It will be seen that this goes back to within three years of the constitution of the first Presbytery. We have little doubt but this is a correct statement. We have no other, reliable one which antedates it, and therefore we shall assume this as the beginning corner of the Cumberland Presbyterian Church in Illinois. It will also be seen from the statement of Mr. Crawford that the first seed was planted by a true son of the Church. Dr. Beard, in his biography of Mr. Barnett, says he was "licensed to preach by Logan Presbytery, August 31, 1813, and ordained August 11, 1815." And as Mr. Crawford dates Mr. Barnett's first visit across the Ohio in the same year, it must have been but a short time after his ordination. It would seem from this that the new kind of Presbyterians was introduced into Illinois prior to its entering Missouri. The first Cumberland Presbyterian minister who removed to, and *settled in*, Illinois, or, indeed, any where north of the Ohio River, seems to have been Rev. Green P. Rice.

Judge R. C. Ewing, in "Historical Memoirs," says (page 11), "The most accurate information to which I have access is to the effect that Rev. Green P. Rice moved to Western Illinois as early as 1817. He came to St. Louis and preached in the then small French village, and was frequently in Missouri attending the Presbyteries during the first years of the Church." When McGee Presbytery, in Missouri, was formed it contained the western part of Illinois, and all of Missouri and Arkansas, and at its first meeting (1820) the only minister recorded or belonging to it in Illinois was Mr. Rice, who was present. This meeting was held in Pike county, Missouri, in the spring of that year, and was composed of Revs. Daniel Buie and R. D. Morrow, of Missouri, Rev. Green P. Rice, of Illinois, and Rev. John Carnahan, of Arkansas. Mr. Rice resided in what is now Bond, but was then Madison county, for several years, and when Bond county was stricken off and organized, its county seat is said to have been named for him or in honor of his first name, and hence is called Greenville. Mr. Rice came to Illinois from the Southern States, and finally returned to the South, and rumor said, became somewhat dissipated in the latter part of his life. When or where he died is unknown to the writer.

The next minister who became a resident of the State was Rev. David W. McLin. In the life of Rev. Joel Knight, as written by himself, we find the following passage: "Rev. David W. McLin had settled during the preceding fall at Seven Mile Prairie, White county, Illinois. There I selected a place, and in the spring of 1819 I reached the place with my family."—[*Our Faith*, May, 1876. This would say that Mr. McLin's settlement was in the fall of 1818. Mr. Knight also records a "communion meeting" in August of the same year (1819)— he does not say a camp-meeting—"at Hopewell," which was in his neighborhood, at which he says, "Revs. William Barnett, John Barnett, William Henry, Dr. Johnson, a licentiate, and Aaron Shelby attended." The meeting lasted several days, and in all probability was a camp-meeting, for a several days' meeting was never held in those days without a portion of the people remaining in tents or camps on the ground.

#### FIRST CAMP-MEETING.

From a variety of somewhat conflicting accounts, I am, however, persuaded that the *first* camp-meeting ever held in the State was near where Edwardsville now stands, in Madison county. I get this information from W. P. B. Paisley, of Emporia, Kansas, whose father camped on the ground, and indeed was the means of the meeting being held. I will let Mr. Paisley speak for himself. His letter is dated Emporia, Kansas, November 28, 1876. He says: "The first camp-meeting held by Cumberland Presbyterians in Illinois was held in Madison county, two miles south of Edwardsville, at the old Ebenezer Camp Ground, in September of the year 1817. Ministers, Revs. William Barnett and Green Prior Rice. The second camp-meeting (in this part of the State) was held in June, 1819, in the timber, about two miles southwest of the place now called Elm Point, in Bond county. Ministers, G. P. Rice, Robert Morrow and John Carnahan.

The third camp-meeting was in the fall of 1820, about one mile northeast of where the second was held. Ministers, Rice, Morrow and William Long." That Mr. Paisley is correct about the *first* camp-meeting, and perhaps the second, there can be little doubt. We have none else reported as being held so early. But the third meeting is called in question by Mr. Knight.

A very interesting and reliable paper has also been furnished us, already alluded to, from a very venerable father in Israel who still lingers on the shores of time, and whose memory goes back with vividness to the beginning of our efforts in this Territory, as it then was. We refer to Rev. John Crawford, Ridgeway, Ill., now more than three score and ten. We will let him speak for himself:

"In presenting a condensed sketch of the introduction of Cumberland Presbyterians into that part of Southern Illinois now occupied by Illinois Presbytery, I will first state that I was born in South Carolina, January 31st, 1804, and that my father, John Crawford, with Grandfather Glass and other families, all Presbyterians, emigrated to the bank of the Ohio River, on the Kentucky shore, nearly opposite the present site of Golconda, in the fall of 1805. My father crossed into Illinois Territory, and located at the mouth of Grandpear Creek, in sight of an Indian encampment of about thirty, a hunting party, in the year 1808. Shortly after Francis Glass, an elder, crossed to Illinois and located two miles northwest of present site of Golconda; his daughter, Elizabeth, having married Robert Tagert, near Clarksville, Tenn., they were both converted and inducted into the Cumberland Presbyterian Church under the administration of Finis Ewing, by whom their first born, Nancy R., was baptized. Mr. Tagert, being a surveyor, removed to Illinois to engage in that business, in the year 1813. I think they were the first Cumberland Presbyterians that crossed the Ohio River. He died at Mr. Glass' the same year, where the first sermon by a Cumberland

Presbyterian minister, the Rev. John Barnett, was preached in that part of Illinois in the year 1815. As Mr. Glass' sympathies were with the revival measures, his house was a stand for Cumberland Presbyterian preaching to his death, and all the younger members of his family were converted under their efforts.

"The Rev. Darrow, an Old School divine, had breathed the spirit of Craighead into my father's house by warning them of the danger of the Cumberland Presbyterians. About this time, in the year 1816, Dr. James Johnson, at the request of my oldest brother, who had been converted under his preaching in Kentucky, sent an appointment to my father's house, which was received with some fearful apprehensions. When the sermon closed the Doctor began to sing praise to God with much feeling, and to extend a warm hand to his audience, when my parents fled and signaled their numerous household to imitate, which was done. The Doctor didn't leave any appointment to preach again. It is due my parents to state that, when the power of God, through the preaching of these men, had brought several of their children to Christ and to membership in the Cumberland Presbyterian Church, the spirit of Craighead departed from them. I heard Ewing at Golconda, on his way to Missouri, date not known.

"The first camp-meeting was held at Sugar Creek, Pope county, by Revs. John Barnett, Aaron Shelby and James Johnson, September, 1821. At this meeting Nancy Tagert, Joseph Glass and others were converted and a church organized—Elders, Joseph Wilson, Israel Boazarth, —— Robinson and James Crawford.

"I heard Thomas Campbell, of Kentucky, as he passed to Sangamon county, in the summer of 1822. This was the beginning of my serious impressions. I was in great trouble until Sabbath night of a camp-meeting at Sugar Creek, same fall, when Christ appeared to me as one altogether lovely. Ministers in attendance, Aaron Shelby, William Henry and

Hiram McDaniel. About this time Revs. Thomas Long and Frank Braley, in passing from Tennessee to Missouri, preached in Union county. A circuit was also formed, embracing all the river counties, and supplied from Kentucky by Gilbert Dodds, Thomas Boan and William McClusky; afterwards from Illinois Presbytery by Nimrod G. Ferguson and James S. Alexander. For many years this has been a missionary field affording but little support to the laborer. It has been partially cultivated by other faithful ministers who have gone to their reward, of whom were D. W. McLin, Jesse Pearce, W. M. Hamilton, John Porter, Richard Harris and William Davis. At one time, when no minister lived in said boundary, J. S. Alexander and I volunteered a joint effort of fourteen days and nights. Result: over 100 professions and the organization of two congregations that remain permanent. That field is now occupied by a class of self-sacrificing, devout men, of whom are Revs. Wells, Eldridge, Jordan, Simpson, Mangrum and Thompson, with several young men coming up to the work."

### RECAPITULATION.

Rev. Joel Knight says (Sketches of Early History of the Church in Illinois, C. P., 1873,) "that Rev. David W. McLin settled at Seven Mile Prairie, White county, Illinois, in 1818." This would make Mr. Rice's settlement in Madison (now Bond) county, according to "Historical Memoirs," at least one year previous. So it seems we have from Rev. Mr. Crawford that the first sermon preached on Illinois soil by a Cumberland Presbyterian, was preached as early as 1815, by Rev. John Barnett at the house of Francis Glass, near the present site of Golconda—and the first Cumberland Presbyterian family which entered the Territory to reside was Mr. and Mrs. Tagert, the son-in-law and daughter of Mr. Glass. That was in 1813, just three years after the Cumberland Presbytery was organized. And Mr. Paisley tells us that the first camp-meeting ever held in the State was at the old Methodist camp-ground, called Ebenezer, a short distance southwest of Edwardsville, county seat of Madison county, by Revs. William Barnett and G. P. Rice, in September, 1817. There was no organization of a congregation at this meeting.

### FIRST CONGREGATION.

The first *congregation* organized in the State seems to have been Hopewell, now Enfield, in White county, by Rev. D. W. McLin, June 8, 1819. This is taken from their own records. Mr. Knight, in his "Sketches," says a camp-meeting was held there (Hopewell) in August of that same year "which was truly a success to many, and myself, one of that number. I came to the State under great distress of mind, but at that meeting a soul-satisfying view of the plan of salvation, brought that peace which Jesus alone by the Spirit can communicate. At this meeting Mr. McLin had the assistance of Revs. John Barnett, William Henry, Dr. Johnson, a licentiate, and Aaron Shelby, a candidate." He also tells us that Mr. McLin and his people "had built a large log meeting-house here, previous to their camp-meeting. The house was covered but not floored." In all probability this was the first church-house built by our people in Illinois. It is pleasing to know that this congregation, after an existence of more than half a century, is still in a flourishing condition, having our estimable brother, Rev. J. M. Miller, as pastor. He is the son of James Miller, who held the office of Ruling Elder from the day of his appointment at the organization of the congregation to the day of his death about forty years ago. His son, Rev. J. M. Miller, has been the successful pastor of this congregation for more than thirty-two years.

At its organization, the following were set apart to the office of Eldership: James Mays, Samuel Craig and James

Miller. Soon after, Lawrence Rolofson, J. C. Goudy and Robert Goudy were added. Later, William Orr (yet living but super-annuated—82 years old), William Goudy (dead), D. W. Jamison (dead), J. M. Fields (dead). The present Board of Elders are M. A. Miller, P. M. Orr, P. A. Orr, J. M. Miller, Jr., and John Tarrentine. They have a good church building out of debt, a congregation in good working order, with a live Sabbath school; and, indeed, they are exhibiting all the symptoms of life and vigor. It is exceedingly pleasant to be permitted to note such a fact, after the fluctuations of half a century in this exceedingly fluctuating country, that on the spot where our fathers organized the first church in Illinois, and set the wheels in motion, they are found running on with ease and in harmony sixty years afterward.

The reader will also remember that the first sermon was preached near the present town of Golconda, and that in that community, likewise, Cumberland Presbyterians still hold a respectable influence after the lapse of three score years. The results of the first camp-meeting, too, are visible to the present day. Our informant, Mr. Paisley, says there was only one conversion at the meeting, and that "a colored man;" no church organized or attempted to be organized; but yet such were the seed sown and the happy influences resulting therefrom, that they are plainly visible to-day. The causes which brought about this first camp-meeting near Edwardsville I will let Mr. Paisley tell in his own language, merely stating that the writer has been on the spot of ground many a time, and the old church and a remnant of the camp-ground are still standing on the same spot. It is about eight miles south-east of the city of Alton, which was our field of labor for more than nineteen years. Mr. Paisley says:

"When my father first moved to Illinois he stopped at or near Edwardsville, Madison county, where the Robinsons, Barbers, and others of the Old Presbyterians, as they were then called, and a few Methodists had settled. Nearly all of them were subjects of the revival of 1800, but were not of the same country. There was none of them but a few of the Methodists that knew anything of the Cumberland Presbyterians, but they were religious, and they soon started a prayer-meeting. While at the prayer-meeting, in view of the destitution of the means of grace, they entered into a covenant verbally to pray for a revival of religion, and for some one to break to them the bread of life, agreeing to receive and sustain the first one that should come. Father, knowing that he could not be satisfied with any but a Cumberland Presbyterian, as soon as he could, sat down and wrote to Rev. Wm. Barnett just the situation he was in, and his great anxiety to have Cumberland Presbyterian preaching. He never told any one what he had done. In some three or four weeks he got notice that Mr. Barnett would be there, and that in three or four days, and would hold a camp-meeting. He urged father to be ready. That is why the meeting was at the Methodist camp-ground near Edwardsville. There was a strong prejudice against them by those that knew nothing of them, but it was not long till the most of it was gone. Father Barber and the two Robinson families, Joseph's and David's, were reconciled and converted to Cumberlandism. I have heard quite a number of anecdotes of their fears and prejudices, and how they got clear of them. Some of them are real amusing. There was no church organized there at that time, though there was material enough if they had stuck together. I think there was one profession of religion at that meeting—a colored man. Rev. Rice was a man of considerable ability as a preacher, but he let the world get the upper hand of him, and his usefulness was lost to the church. He was at the camp-meeting above named."

At the risk of repeating somewhat, we will give the version of this camp-meeting as related in the "Sketches" of Rev.

Joel Knight, as it throws additional light upon an incident which must be of great interest to all who love to read of God's guidance of, and care for, his true disciples. Mr. Knight says ("Sketches," August 8, 1873):

"Some time previous to the time that Mr. McLin settled in White county, Mr. Robert Paisley, a Cumberland Presbyterian from Rev. Finis Ewing's congregation in Kentucky, had settled, with his family, in Madison county, Ill. John Barber, Joseph Robinson, and some other families of revival Presbyterians, lived in the same vicinity. They all united in forming a prayer-meeting, which became quite interesting. Revival Christians in those days could talk, exhort, encourage Christians, warn sinners, urge them to flee from the wrath to come, call them forward to be prayed for, instruct and labor for their salvation. Well, they agreed that if a Cumberland Presbyterian minister should be the first that came to preach to them that they would all join, &c. That was a matter of great interest with Mr. Paisley, in view of the religious situation of that community. He wrote to Rev. Wm. Barnett, of Kentucky, expressing the ardent feelings of his very heart, and requested him to attend a meeting with them, appoint a camp-meeting, and give them one meeting at the least. Mr. Barnett told Rev. Finis Ewing of this letter, expressed the feelings he had on the subject, and said if he had a suitable horse and rigging he felt like he would go. Mr. Ewing told him if he would furnish him with that letter he would fit him out. He furnished it. The next Sabbath, after preaching, Mr. Ewing read the letter to the congregation, and told them the object was to raise means to fit out Mr. Barnett with a good horse and equipage, so that he might meet the request. The money was promptly raised, and Mr. Ewing had Mr. Barnett completely fitted out for the trip, and in due time he accomplished it. In those days Cumberland preachers did not ride in buggies. But we see that through the influence of Mr. Paisley, Rev. Mr. Barnett was induced to appoint and attend a camp-meeting in that part of the then new West. The meeting was a success in the new country, and out of its influence grew up the Goshen congregation (now Columbia). Mr. Barber's family, and two of the Messrs. Robinson families, constituted the pillars of that congregation, but the other Presbyterians never joined.

"After that Rev. Green P. Rice moved into that region of the country and preached to them a short time; subsequently to St. Louis, and finally to Bond county, and settled where the county seat was located, and it was called Greenville for him.

"Mr. Paisley also moved and settled on the north side of Bond county. Here Mr. Rice organized a congregation by the name of Bear Creek. Robert Paisley and John Kirkpatrick were the first ruling elders. Part of the membership was in Bond and part in Montgomery counties."

### THE SECOND CHURCH.

The writer is satisfied that this was the second congregation of Cumberland Presbyterians organized in what is now the State of Illinois, and Mr. Paisley says it was organized out of the persons who attended that prayer-meeting, and was the result of the first camp-meeting already referred to. He further says, in a letter to the writer, that this congregation was organized by Rev. Mr. Rice "at the house of William Robinson, some three miles north of Greenville. The first members were father and mother, Jonathan Berry and wife, William Young and wife—just six in all. Mr. Thomas Elison and wife joined soon after. In the course of twelve or eighteen months Mr. Joseph Williams and wife, John Kirkpatrick and family joined. This organization was in 1818 or 1819, and was the start of Bear Creek church, now at Donnellson, Montgomery county, Ill."

I feel sure that this organization was in 1819. This

congregation for some years embraced the membership of what is now Madison, Bond and Montgomery counties.

### EARLY DAYS—AN INCIDENT.

In looking over the early days of the Church of Christ in this country, and of the efforts of Presbyterianism in particular, a friend has called my attention to the following item, found in the "Life and Times of Rev. Stephen Bliss," a pioneer minister of the Presbyterian Church. We are sure all Cumberland Presbyterians will be interested in it. It says: "In 1810 or 1811 the Rev. James McGready, of the Muhlenberg Presbytery, Ky., made missionary tours into Southern Indiana, and having penetrated into Illinois as far as White county to a settlement of emigrants from the Carolinas, Georgia, Tennessee and Kentucky, he organized the Sharon church in 1816. This is the oldest Presbyterian, and, so far as known, the oldest Protestant church in the State."

Two points in this statement are of intense interest to us, if true: First, that the "mother Church" entered the territory of Illinois and organized a church but one year in advance of the cast-off daughter. Second, that this first Presbyterian church was the result of the labors of Rev. Mr. McGready, who, under God, was the main instrument of the revival influences out of which grew the Cumberland Presbyterian Church. So the strong and powerful Presbyterian Church in Illinois is indebted, for their first organized church in the State, to the enterprise of that man whom Kentucky Synod suspended from the ministry for endorsing the revival measures, and sympathizing with the fathers, doctrines and measures of the Cumberland Presbyterians.

From these two small beginnings—Hopewell in White county and Bear Creek in Madison (now Bond) county— have sprung, in less than sixty years, the ten Presbyteries, three Synods, and more than a hundred and fifty congregations which are now scattered over the State. Mr. Knight refers to Goshen congregation, and to the fact that "a part of the membership" of this Bear Creek congregation "was in Bond and a part in Montgomery counties." The part of them near Edwardsville was organized, not long after this, into the old Goshen church; and the first meeting the writer ever attended in the State of Illinois was at this old church house. It stood about three miles south-east of the town. This was in the Spring or Summer of 1853. Removals and deaths have greatly thinned their numbers, but the congregation still exists, holding its place of worship a few miles east of Edwardsville, where they have a neat and comfortable chapel. The congregation includes some of the leading and most influential citizens in the county.

It is a pleasing fact to record, that at all the points where Cumberland Presbyterians first organized their work in the Territory or State, they have held their ground and made creditable advancement.

# CHAPTER II.

FIRST PRESBYTERY—WHEN, WHERE, AND BY WHOM ORGANIZED—ITS SUBSEQUENT HISTORY FOR SEVERAL YEARS.

It must be remembered that a part of Illinois—the Western part—was, by action of the old Cumberland Synod, made a part of McGee Presbytery. This Presbytery, therefore, held Rev. Mr. Rice as a member, while Mr. McLin still held his membership in Logan Presbytery (until Anderson was stricken off), which at one time covered all Indiana and the east half of Illinois, as well as all Kentucky.

## M<sup>c</sup>GEE PRESBYTERY,

the first Presbytery west of the Mississippi, was organized in Pike county, Mo., in the Spring of 1820. "The first members were Rice, of Illinois, Morrow (R. D.) and Buie, of Missouri, and John Carnahan, of Arkansas."—Historical Sketches, page 12. Three years after this the Presbytery of Illinois was organized, according to a previous order of Synod. We will let Mr. Knight tell the story in his own words, as he was present as a licensed preacher. He wrote in 1873:

"In the Fall of 1822, the Synod passed an order for the State of Illinois to be stricken off from Anderson Presbytery,* and for Illinois Presbytery to be formed the succeeding Spring, in May, in Mr. Rice's congregation (Bear Creek). Mr. Rice was to be the first Moderator, and, in case he

---

* Father Knight is mistaken about the entire State of Illinois being in Anderson Presbytery. A part was in McGee Presbytery, as the order for the organization of the new Presbytery will show.—[Ed.

should be absent, then Mr. McLin. Mr. Rice was at that time on a visit South with his family, and never returned.

"A camp-meeting was appointed to immediately precede the organization of the Presbytery. The ordained ministers, except Mr. Rice, all attended. The writer was a licentiate and also attended. Vandalia, then a mere village on the bank of Oakaw (Kaskaskia) river, was then the seat of government in the State of Illinois. Messrs. McLin, Hamilton, I think, one or two elders and myself, traveled from White county. When we got to the bottom land of the river, it was all covered with water so deep as to be dangerous for strangers to cross. We hired a pilot. When we got to the bed of the river there was a little dry land on the bank where we could dismount, take off our rigging, then swim our horses across, one at a time, by the side of a skiff, and then we were in Vandalia.

"The meeting in this wild country in the Spring of the year was a good one. Many professed religion who became church members. When the meeting closed, on Tuesday morning we repaired across the prairie about three miles to the house of John Kirkpatrick, and there constituted and organized Illinois Presbytery in May, 1823. Rev. Messrs. David W. McLin, John M. Berry and Woods M. Hamilton, being all the ministers then in the State, were all present. When the first meeting of Illinois Presbytery closed, it adjourned to meet in a congregation a short distance north of Shawneetown, Gallatin county, Ill. But before it closed, an order was passed for the ordination of Jesse Pearce, and an intermediate Presbytery to meet in Hopewell congregation at the camp-meeting in August for that purpose. When the time came Mr. Pearce was ordained. Besides other business, the writer was ordered to form a circuit, including Bear Creek in the eastern part, and to extend as far west as Edwardsville, in Madison county. A camp-meeting was also appointed to be held in Bond county, some four miles northwest of Greenville, and I was directed to collect what material I could and have them ready for organization at the camp-meeting, which was done to the best of my ability. At the meeting the congregation was organized, bearing the name of Mt. Gilead."

I have been kindly furnished the minutes of this Presbytery for all the years until it was divided. I deem it of sufficient interest to copy the first minutes entire. The book in which these minutes are kept is in excellent preservation. The first minutes are in a clear, bold, plain hand, and are just as the Clerk left them more than fifty-five years since. I have had an inexpressibly sad and strange pleasure in handling these pages, and reading after the venerable and godly men whose acts are herein recorded. Every one of those taking any part in that Presbyterial meeting, so far as I know, have gone to their reward. How little did they dream that, when they met in that unpretending log cabin on that beautiful May morning in that then wild, wilderness country, they were setting in motion an agency which, notwithstanding their poverty and lack of worldly fame, would, in half a century, be multiplied more than ten fold in the membership of the Church, and a hundred fold in other elements of power and influences for good, as will be seen in the sequel.

Before proceeding to quote from the records of the Presbytery, I must say a few words about Rev. J. M. Berry and his work. We have already seen that Rev. Messrs. McLin and Hamilton had settled in White county, in the south-eastern portion of the State, and Rev. Mr. Rice in the south-western portion, in Madison, and afterwards in Bond county. Rev. John M. Berry, when he came into the State, settled in what was called the Sangamon country, in the northern part of the settled portion of the State, not far from Springfield, the present Capital. He was an active, energetic, and very successful minister. Soon large and flourishing churches sprang up all over his territory of operations.

## THE FIRST CHURCH NORTH.

Among the first, if not the first organized congregation in the Sangamon country, was Sugar Creek church, which is still in existence, about ten miles south of Springfield. The old-time church house has been replaced by a beautiful, large, and commodious building of modern shape and finish, which has a large, intelligent, and pious membership surrounding, filling it to overflowing at the regular periods for worship. It has been my privilege to worship with them on several occasions, and therefore I can speak from personal knowledge. But to the Presbytery.

I find on the record of this Presbytery for many years, beginning with its organization, a notice of "elders" present, and also of "representatives" present. Knowing that all "representatives" were elders, I have been puzzled to know just why "elders" who were not "representatives" should be taken notice of at all. I have surmised, but do not know, that, being young and weak, they welcomed the presence and *counsel* of all elders who might attend, but did not regard them as actual members. If this is not the solution of this matter, then the reader must solve it for himself.

## ORGANIZING THE PRESBYTERY.

"Whereas, the Cumberland Synod of the Cumberland Presbyterian Church, at the session of 1822, ordered a Presbytery to be stricken off from Anderson and McGee Presbyteries, to be known by the name of Illinois Presbytery, including the State of Illinois;

"Agreeable to the order of Synod, the Illinois Presbytery met on the first Tuesday in May, 1823, at the house of John Kirkpatrick, Montgomery county, State of Illinois. Opened by a sermon delivered by Rev. David W. McLin, from second epistle to Timothy, 4th chapter and 2d verse. Constituted by prayer. Members present: the Revs. Messrs. David W. McLin, John M. Berry and Woods M. Hamilton.

Absent: Green P. Rice. Elders: John Hamilton, John Kirkpatrick and John M. Cameron.

"John M. Berry was chosen Moderator, and Woods M. Hamilton Clerk.

"Gilbert Dodds, Thomas Bone, Nimrod G. Ferguson, Joel Knight, Jesse Pearce, and John Porter, licentiates, and Benjamin Bruce, John Files, and John Pearce, candidates, having been dismissed from the Anderson Presbytery, and by them recommended to the care of the Illinois Presbytery,

"*Resolved*, That the above named licentiates and candidates be considered under the care of Presbytery.

"Ordered that each licentiate and candidate attend Presbytery from time to time, to be examined on English Grammar and Divinity.

"Synod having passed an order that each Presbytery report to Synod on the state of religion annually, therefore, to possess this Presbytery of the information necessary to compose their report, *Resolved*, that each ordained preacher and licentiate keep a journal, and make a report of the state of religion within the bounds where he preaches to each Presbytery.

"Robert Paisley, representative from Bear Creek society, attended and took his seat.

"*Resolved*, That the following Preamble and Constitution be recommended to the societies under the care of this Presbytery:

"The Illinois Presbytery, taking into view the necessity of missionary labors, recommend to the organized, enrolled societies under her care to form missionary societies, the object of which is to raise funds for the support of missionaries within the bounds of this Presbytery.

"FORM OF THE PROPOSED CONSTITUTION.

"ARTICLE I.—We, the undersigned, agree to form ourselves into a society, to be known as ———— Missionary Society.

"Article 2.—Each member shall contribute the sum annexed to his or her name, respectively, twice a year.

"Article 3.—This Society shall, at their first meeting, choose a Treasurer, whose duty it shall be to receive all moneys of the Society, and transmit the same to Presbytery at each session.

"Article 4.—The Illinois Presbytery is hereby constituted a Board of Missions, and shall distribute the moneys received from this Society to her missionaries at discretion.

"Article 5.—Any member may withdraw at pleasure, paying arrearages.

"The Synod having passed an order requiring each Presbytery to adopt some measure to coerce the attendance of elders at Synod; therefore *Resolved*, that each ordained preacher, in the Society or Societies where he preaches, shall appoint two elders, who shall hold themselves in readiness to attend Synod, one of whom shall be first named, on whom the duty shall devolve, unless providentially prevented. In such case the duty shall devolve on the other; and if either should refuse, he shall be dealt with as contumacious.

"Ordered that Nimrod G. Ferguson ride and preach the whole of his time on the Golconda district until our next Presbytery; Thomas Bone the whole of his time on the Shawneetown district; and Joel Knight three months on the Shoal Creek district.

"*Resolved*, That the Saturday before the first Sabbath in June next be observed throughout the bounds of the Illinois Presbytery as a day of fasting and prayer, the object of which is, that the Lord may revive his work, and call and send forth laborers into his vineyard.

"Presbytery adjourned to meet to-morrow morning at seven o'clock. Concluded with prayer.

"Wednesday morning, Presbytery met agreeable to adjournment. Constituted by prayer. Members present as on yesterday, except Robert Paisley.

"Benjamin Bruce read a discourse from a text previously assigned him by the Anderson Presbytery, which was sustained as a part of trial. Ordered that Benjamin Bruce prepare a written discourse from John, 3d chapter and 7th verse; John Files from 1st Peter, 4th chapter, 18th verse; and John Pearce from Luke, 13th chapter, 5th verse, to be read at our next Presbytery.

"Presbytery examined John M. Cameron and Josiah Kirkpatrick on their knowledge of experimental religion, and their internal call and motives to the ministry; which examinations were sustained. Their moral characters standing fair, and they being in communion of the Church, were received as candidates for the work of the ministry. Ordered that John M. Cameron prepare a written discourse from Amos, 4th chapter, last part of 12th verse, and Josiah Kirkpatrick from John, 9th chapter, last part of the 25th verse, to be read at our next Presbytery.

"Robert Paisley attended and took his seat, whose excuse for absence was sustained.

"Ordered that John M. Berry, David W. McLin and Woods M. Hamilton meet at Hopewell meeting-house, White county, State of Illinois, on the Friday before the first Sabbath in August next, and constitute an intermediate Presbytery for the purpose of ordaining Jesse Pearce, and that he deliver a discourse from Romans, 10th chapter, 4th verse, and prepare to be examined on the different branches required by Discipline preparatory to ordination; that John M. Berry preach the ordination sermon, and David W. McLin preside and give the charge.

"Ordered that Woods M. Hamilton be, and he is hereby appointed Stated Clerk.

"Ordered that each ordained preacher attend to public examinations in the organized Societies within our bounds once a year.

"Presbytery adjourned to meet at New Salem meeting

house, Gallatin county, State of Illinois, on the second Tuesday in October, 1823. Concluded with prayer.

"JOHN M. BERRY, Moderator.
"WOODS M. HAMILTON, Clerk."

We have given this minute entire and *verbatim*, that the reader may see the spirit of the men who, under God, first planted the Cumberland Presbyterian Church in the State of Illinois. With two of the ordained ministers comprising this Presbytery it was my pleasure to be acquainted personally; to-wit, Mr. Berry and Mr. Hamilton. Mr. McLin died before my acquaintance in the State. Mr. Berry was a strong-minded, resolute, bold, and very successful minister, whose praise was in all the churches. Mr. Hamilton was a man universally beloved, and in the first part of his ministry, as well as in the latter part, he was greatly useful. For a few years at one time he was suspended from the ministry; but such was his humble walk and Godly conversation during this season that he won the confidence of even his enemies; and his neighbors—members of different churches and the outside world—all joined in an urgent petition to Presbytery to remove the suspension. It was done; and to the close of a long life he never gave any one cause to regret the confidence thus reposed in him. Mr. McLin was not inferior to either of the others mentioned. He seems to have been a man of strong convictions, great resolution, and constant devotion to his Master's cause. He was greatly successful. We shall have more to record in another place of all these noble men.

I may mention, also, that the place where this organization and meeting was held is now about the geographical center of Vandalia Presbytery, the field where God in his providence has placed the writer for more than twenty years; and it is pleasing to note that around that spot of ground in all directions are Cumberland Presbyterian churches: our people being more numerous in that county than in any other in the State, with, perhaps, one exception. It has been my privilege to preach at old Bear Creek church many a time. It is one of the strongest in the Presbytery, having a good brick church house, a worthy pastor, and an efficient Sunday-school and membership.

Of all who attended this Presbytery, either as ministers, elders, or candidates, not one is living, except Rev. J. M. Cameron, who, as we have seen, became a candidate for the ministry at this Presbytery. At last accounts he was living at Sebastopol, California, a very old man.*

All these were pre-eminently self-sacrificing men. They loved souls, and did an immense amount of labor for very little pay in the treasures of this world. But they were men "rich in faith," "strong in the Lord and in the power of his might."

### FIRST MINISTER ORDAINED.

As we have seen, an intermediate Presbytery was appointed, at which Rev. Jesse Pearce was ordained. He was, therefore, the first man set apart by Cumberland Presbyterians to the whole work of the ministry on the soil of Illinois. The session was at old Hopewell, White county. John M. Berry was Moderator, Woods M. Hamilton Clerk; and the ordination took place August 1, 1823.

### SUBSEQUENT MEETINGS.

The next regular meeting was held at New Salem meeting house, Gallatin county, Illinois, on October 14th, 1823. Members present: Berry, McLin, and Hamilton; Absent: G. P. Rice. The opening sermon was preached by Mr. McLin. Elders present: Payton Mitchell, James Miller and John Files. Representatives: John Kirkpatrick from Bear Creek, Joseph M. Street from New Salem, John Barber from Mt. Gilead, and Richard Harris from Village Society.

*Mr. Cameron has died since the above was written.—ED.

Mr. Berry was Moderator and Mr. Hamilton Clerk. Jesse Pearce was invited and took a seat for the first time as a member. At this meeting John Barber, Payton Mitchell, James E. Davis and James T. Alexander were received as candidates for the ministry. Green P. Rice, by letter, requested a letter of dismission and recommendation to some Presbytery South, which was granted. Benjamin Bruce, John M. Cameron and John Files read discourses, which were sustained as parts of trial. At this meeting we find Rev. David Foster present from Nashville Presbytery, and invited to a seat in counsel. Jesse Pearce was ordered to ride and preach the whole of his time in the Golconda district. On the last day of Presbytery two more candidates were received—John W. McCord and Richard Harris. An order was passed for the ordination of Joel Knight at next session of Presbytery. Thomas Bone, licentiate, was dismissed by letter at his request. Joel Knight and Thomas Bone had filled the missions assigned, and Nimrod G. Ferguson had ridden but two months, on account of sickness. His excuse was sustained. A committee was appointed to draft a circular letter to all the churches; but we are not told who the committee were, nor is a copy of the letter retained.

The next meeting was at the house of James Johnson, Bond county, April 6, 1824. Ministers present: McLin, Hamilton, Pearce and Berry. Elders: James Miller, Samuel Hill, Henry Grimes and John M. Cameron. Representatives: Richard Harris from Village, John Files from Shiloh, Robert Paisley from Bear Creek, and Thomas Hunter from Mt. Gilead Societies. Mr. Pearce was Moderator and Mr. Berry Clerk. Joel Knight and Nimrod G. Ferguson were set apart to the whole work of the ministry. Mr. Hamilton preached the ordination sermon, and Mr. McLin gave the charge. John Knight and Thomas Hunter were received as candidates for the ministry. John Barber and John W. McCord were licensed to preach the gospel. Mr. Ferguson was to preach all his time in the Golconda district; Mr. McCord three months in the Shawneetown district; Mr. Barber four months in the Shoal Creek district; and Mr. Porter two months in the Sangamon district. The second Saturdays in June and August were set apart as days of fasting and prayer.

The next meeting was at Hopewell meeting house, White county, October 5th, 1824. Ministers present: McLin, Hamilton, Berry, Pearce, Knight and Ferguson. Six elders were present, and three representatives. Mr. Knight was Moderator, and Mr. Ferguson Clerk—both placed in office at the first meeting of Presbytery after their ordination. Eight candidates read discourses, which were sustained as parts of trial. Thomas Campbell, a licentiate from the Anderson Presbytery, was received by letter and his name placed on the roll. Alexander F. Trousdale, Marmaduke S. Ferguson and William Davis were received as candidates. Mr. Pearce was ordered to ride and preach two months in the Golconda district, and Mr. Hamilton two months in the Shawneetown district.

The Spring session of 1825 met at Bear Creek church, Montgomery county. Ministers present: McLin, Hamilton, Berry, Pearce, Knight, and Ferguson; elders, five; representatives, four. Mr. Ferguson was the Moderator and Mr. Knight Clerk. An intermediate Presbytery had been appointed for the purpose of ordaining Thomas Campbell, but it failed of a quorum, and Mr. Campbell was ordained at this session. Mr. McLin preached the ordination sermon and gave the charge also. Neill Johnson was received as a candidate for the ministry at this session. Inquiry was made if the order had been complied with about catechising or holding public examinations on the Shorter Catechism. All reported compliance but one, and his excuse was sustained. Benjamin Bruce, James T. Alexander and John Knight were licensed to preach the gospel, and all put upon circuits.

The Fall session of Presbytery met October 11, 1824, at Village church, White county. Present: McLin, Berry, Hamilton and Knight. Absent: Ferguson and Campbell. Elders five and representatives five. Mr. Berry was Moderator and Hamilton Clerk. John W. McCord was granted a letter of dismission and recommendation. Here came up the first reference of a trial case upon which the advice of the Presbytery was asked. It was from Hopewell society, and about a man charged with "perjury." The Presbytery decided, from the evidence submitted, that the man was guilty, and advised the church to act toward him accordingly. John Files, a candidate, is here kindly dismissed, the Presbytery believing his calling and gifts were only to "exhort;" and they tenderly advise him accordingly,

### SHALL THERE BE A GENERAL ASSEMBLY?

At this session we find the Presbytery acting upon what form of government the Church should have in the future, as the question had been sent down to them from Cumberland Synod, "Whether they desire a continuation of the present form of government, or form a delegated Synod, or divide the Synod and form a General Assembly." The reader will see the question was three-sided. The Presbytery answered as follows:

"*Resolved*, Therefore, that this Presbytery is of opinion that the state and interest of the Church require a division of the Synod and the formation of a General Assembly."

Another important action was the examination into and acquital of James T. Alexander of a "scandalous report" against his character. They pronounced him "not guilty." Ezekiel Porter and James S. Smith were received as candidates. James E. Davis, Alexander F. Trousdale, Marmaduke S. Ferguson and Richard Harris were licensed to preach.

## TEMPERANCE PLEDGE.

We find the Presbytery at this session placing itself on record in favor of temperance, and against the "evils resulting from the use of ardent spirits," and forming themselves into a temperance society. We very much regret that they did not spread their constitution and pledge upon their records. But it is cheering to find the Cumberland Presbyterians in the front rank of the temperance cause, from its first initiation into the State to the present day. Indeed, we may go further and say, as a denomination they have always been in the front. Their voice, though comparatively feeble, has always been distinct, and by no means uncertain. It has been as common and natural for our preachers to preach temperance as to preach any other Bible truth. Our judicatories everywhere have spoken out in no uncertain sounds on this question.

The Spring session of Presbytery met at the house of Joseph Robinson, in Madison county, the first Tuesday in April, 1826. Present: Berry, McLin, Pearce, Knight. Absent: Hamilton, Ferguson and Campbell. Elders present, two. Rev. Robert Sloan, a member of Arkansas Presbytery, was present and took part as an advisory member. William Finley was received as a candidate for the ministry. Josiah Kirkpatrick, a candidate, was discontinued. "The Presbytery, in examining his case, from the best evidence obtained, were led to conclude that his gift and call were not to preach, and in the spirit of brotherly love" discontinued him. Likewise Thomas Hunter, at his own request, was also discontinued as a candidate. John M. Cameron was licensed, in the usual form, to preach the gospel. John Barber and Gilbert Dodds were ordained to the whole work of the ministry, Mr. McLin preaching the ordination sermon and Mr. Berry presiding and giving the charge. We find the following on this minute, which we transcribe: "Whereas, Synod having passed a resolution that each Presbytery be recommended to request the preachers and sessions to appoint special meetings for the purpose of examining seekers of religion, and others, on the state of their souls, *Resolved*, That each preacher appoint and attend such meetings occasionally, where and when he may think proper." At this session Mr. Knight was Moderator and Mr. Pearce Clerk.

The Fall session of 1826 was held at Hopewell, in White county. Present: McLin, Hamilton, Knight, Barber and Ferguson. Absent: Berry, Campbell, (three times,) Dodds and Pearce. Elders, three. Representatives, four. Mr. Barber was Moderator and Mr. Ferguson Clerk. Rev. David M. Kirkpatrick, a member of McGee Presbytery, being present, took part as an advisory member. David Miller, John Crawford, Anthony L. Hamilton and Samuel Abbott were received as candidates. James S. Smith and Ezekiel Porter, for "satisfactory evidence, were dismissed from under the care of Presbytery."

The Spring session of Presbytery met at Mt. Gilead meeting house, in Bond county, first Monday in March, 1827. Present: McLin, Berry, Hamilton, Knight, Campbell, Barber and Dodds. Absent: Pearce and Ferguson. Representatives, seven. Mr. Berry was Moderator and Mr. Dodds Clerk. At this session John Porter was set apart to the whole work of the ministry. Mr. Berry preached the ordination sermon, Mr. McLin presided, and Mr. Hamilton gave the charge. Stringent rules were adopted to secure prompt attendance of the members, licentiates and candidates.

The Fall session of Presbytery, 1827, met at Hopewell. Present: McLin, Berry, Pearce, Knight, Campbell, Barber and Dodds. Absent: Ferguson and Porter. Representatives, ten. Mr. Campbell was Moderator and Mr. Barber Clerk. At this meeting Rev. David Foster united by letter from Nashville Presbytery.

Here we find the "free, full and open confession" of Woods M. Hamilton to that sin that cast a shadow over all his after-life; and, although he showed signs of deep contrition, he was suspended from exercising any of the functions of the ministry until the Spring session of 1829. This lamentable occurrence was a severe stroke upon the Presbytery and infant denomination, and yet we scarcely know which to admire more—the honesty and frankness of the confession, or the promptness and unanimity with which the Presbytery acted in the case. It was one of those unfortunate mis-steps that good men are sometimes betrayed into making. And yet Mr. Hamilton, in a great measure—perhaps as much so as any person on earth could do—outlived the evil influence of this great wrong, and restored himself to the complete confidence of all who knew him, both in and out of the Church. It was my privilege to have a personal acquaintance with Mr. Hamilton during the later years of his life. I never knew a more humble, unobtrusive, devoted man than he. Never was there anything, not even a shadow, upon his character, covering over a long life, but this one single mistake. He lived and died beloved by all who knew him, and by none more than those who knew him best. There were few, if any, who would have accused him of this wrong, had he not made it known by his own confession. Let, therefore, the broad mantle of charity cover this fault; and let him who would be censorious take care lest he also be tempted.

Jesse Pearce was appointed Stated Clerk instead of Woods M. Hamilton. Mr. Abbott was discontinued as a candidate, because he had joined the "Arian Church." Neill Johnson was licensed to preach the gospel. Archibald Johnson and Samuel Parr were received as candidates for the ministry. Here we find for the first time an attempt at something like a *pastoral* relation between a congregation and a minister. We quote the action in full. All ministerial work, prior to this, had been done by the simple "order" of Presbytery, which was to ride and preach so many months in such a "district." We find these "districts" increasing as we advance. There were Shoal Creek, Shawneetown, Golconda, and Sangamon districts, and even the old preachers were all, up to this time, riding and preaching on these and like districts. Messrs. McLin, Berry, Pearce and others all engaged in this traveling work alike with the younger men. But to the record referred to: "Whereas, Gilbert Dodds, a member of this Presbytery, and William Drennon, a representative from Sugar Creek society, have made known to this Presbytery that there is a contract existing between said parties, which binds the said Dodds to spend one-half of his time in the discharge of his duties as their regular pastor, and that the society is bound, on her part, to liberally contribute for the support of said Dodds, during the existence of said contract. *Resolved*, Therefore, that this Presbytery do hereby approve of said contract."

The Spring session of 1828 convened at William Drennon's, Sugar Creek church, Sangamon county, April 8th, 1828. Present: Foster, Berry, Pearce, Knight, Ferguson, Campbell, Dodds, Barber and Porter. Absent: McLin. Six representatives present. Mr. Dodds was chosen Moderator, and Mr. Campbell Clerk.

At this session Rev. Nimrod G. Ferguson was suspended from all the functions of the ministry. The crime being "buying, removing and selling a person of color, contrary to the laws and statutes of this State in that case made and provided." The proof was "his own voluntary confession."

William McCord, a licentiate from Anderson Presbytery, was received by letter and his name enrolled. We find the following rather strange question acted upon by the Presbytery, which had been referred to them by the Synod: "Whether licentiates and candidates should have a seat in Presbytery and Synod." The answer was, as we would expect: "The Presbytery were unanimously of the opinion that they should not." Contracts were sanctioned for Rev. John Porter to become pastor of Bethel society for one-half his time, and also between Rev. Thomas Campbell and the Spring Creek church for a like proportion of his time as pastor. Joseph Howard and Andrew Finley were received as candidates for the ministry, and William Finley was licensed to preach the gospel of Christ.

The Fall session was held at Shiloh church, in White county, October 9th, 1828. Present: Berry, Pearce, Campbell, Barber, Dodds and Porter. Absent: Foster, McLin and Knight. Eight representatives present. Mr. Porter was Moderator and Mr. Dodds Clerk. William Davis was licensed to preach the gospel. John Barber, Jr., was received as a candidate from under the care of Anderson Presbytery. Daniel Kinchalo was received as a candidate for the ministry.

The Spring session of 1829 met at Bear Creek church, April 14th. Present: McLin, Foster, Berry, Pearce, Campbell and Barber. Absent: Knight, Dodds and Porter. Only three representatives present. Mr. McLin was chosen Moderator and Mr. Barber Clerk. An intermediate Presbytery had been held to license John Barber, Jr., but Mr. Barber had conscientious scruples, and it was not done. Benjamin Bruce, for intoxication, upon his own confession, was suspended from preaching until the next Presbytery. Nimrod G. Ferguson was "restored" to the functions of the ministry. Marmaduke F. Ferguson, a licentiate, obtained a letter of dismission and recommendation.

### THE GENERAL ASSEMBLY.

Here we find the first intimation of the existence of the General Assembly. The record is as follows: "David W. McLin was appointed a commissioner to the General Assembly, which is to be held in Princeton, Caldwell county, Kentucky, on the third Tuesday in May next." The elder delegate was to be appointed as follows: "Ordered that the church sessions of Hopewell and Village societies appoint an elder from one of said societies to the General Assembly, as mentioned in the last section."

It apperars that this was to be the last session in which this noble band of brethren were all to meet together. Cumberland Synod, at its last meeting, had passed an order for the division of Illinois Presbytery, and the formation of a new Presbytery to embrace the more northern part of the State. It was to be called Sangamon, and "John M. Berry, David Foster, Thomas Campbell, Gilbert Dodds and John Porter were appointed to constitute the new Presbytery." It also took the following licentiates under its jurisdiction: John M. Cameron, William McCord and Neill Johnson, together with Payton Mitchell and Archibald Johnson, candidates. John Barber, Jr., was licensed to preach the gospel.

The Fall session of 1829 was held at West Shiloh meetinghouse, Jefferson county, August 27th. Present: McLin, Knight and Barber. Absent: Pearce and Ferguson. Representatives two. Mr. Knight was Moderator, and Mr. Barber Clerk. Mr. McLin reported that he had attended the meeting of the General Assembly, and that an elder had also gone with him as by appointment. Benjamin Bruce was restored to the privilege of preaching again. John Barber, Jr., Benjamin Bruce and William Davis were ordered to ride and preach. Ministers and church sessions were directed to examine the children of the church on the shorter catechism.

The Spring session of 1830 met at Hopewell. Present: McLin, Pearce, Barber and Knight. Absent: Ferguson. Four representatives present. Mr. Pearce was Moderator, and Mr. Knight Clerk. John Barber was the commissioner to the next General Assembly. James S. Alexander was set apart to the whole work of the ministry. The ordination sermon by John Barber, Mr. McLin giving the charge, while Mr. Pearce presided.

The Fall session of 1830 was held in Madison county, on the 14th day of October, at the house of Washington Parkison. Present: Pearce, Knight and Barber. Absent: Ferguson, McLin and Alexander. Four representatives present. Andrew Finley was discontinued as a candidate.

We must now, for a while, take our leave of this old Presbytery. It is much to be regretted, that up to this time we find no report of the state of religion, nor table of statistics. We cannot tell the number of congregations, only as they are represented in the Presbytery. The sessions seem to have been lengthy, but their records are brief. They have had their drawbacks—their dark hours, as we have seen—and yet we can see they have made commendable progress. Already a swarm has gone off to work in another hive, which will be as vigorous as the old one from whence they came. In passing over these pages we are impressed with the following conclusions:

*First*, The church in Illinois was planted by the *fathers* of the church—some of them from old Cumberland Presbytery.

*Second*, They were humble, devoted, self-sacrificing, poor men—men who took delight in serving God, not for mere worldly gain, but to please the Master and advance his cause. Hundreds of miles had to be traversed in attending their camp-meetings and the judicatories of the church, over a sparsely settled country, often with no roads but the open prairies, across swollen streams which had neither ferries nor bridges, and in a country regarded as unusually sickly; and at that period it was not misrepresented in this particular. Often did they swim the streams to get to their appointments. Sometimes a canoe or raft extemporized would bear them over the rushing flood, while their horses were swimming at its side. For the first ten years they had but a few church-houses, preaching mostly in the log cabins of the people, and in the groves of timber in Summer time. What church-houses they had were only small log houses: a brick or a frame building in those days was out of the question.

*Third,* They were men of prayer—every day, constant prayer, full of faith and the Holy Ghost. They did not court or expect worldly applause. They did not attempt to please the people in their sermons. They were plain, pointed, unvarnished. They did not labor for, or expect much reward from men—they evidently looked for their reward from above, and they were not disappointed. Here let me say a word in vindication of the fathers of the Cumberland Presbyterian Church, from the charge often made against them for shunning the towns and inclining only to labor among the country people. It was an absolute necessity on their part. They could not do better. Nor, in point of fact, did they shun the towns. They often preached in them, and were well received, but their facilities, at that day, for building up churches in the towns were so slender, that nine times out of ten it was labor lost if attempted; hence they preferred to labor in the country, where their congregations could live without such close oversight and constant care as a congregation in town would require. As the denomination has grown older and stronger, they have been occupying the towns successfully for years past, and now have flourishing congregations in many towns and smaller cities, and in a few of the great centers of influence and commerce. Let it not be put down as cowardice or conscious personal weakness on their part, that they did not rush into the towns and labor. What were the use of a general, with a mere handful of men, undertaking to storm Gibraltar? He would show his folly, not his wisdom, by the undertaking. Let him wait until his forces are so strengthened that he can successfully make the assault. Nor does it prove anything against his cause that he may, for the time being, be somewhat chary of such fortified places.

*Fourth,* It will appear that Cumberland Presbyterian preachers first came to Illinois at the earnest invitation of members of the Church who had moved into the country.

Here we find a noble example worthy of imitation by all those similarly situated. Instead of plunging out into the wilderness and leaving the church and its blessings behind them, or satisfying themselves with uniting with some other Church, these Cumberland Presbyterian pioneers carried their Church with them, *in their hearts*, and they never rested until they wrote back, and their earnest pleadings brought the Barnetts, Johnson, McLin, Berry and others to the new country with the story of the cross, which fell from their lips with such power and zeal, that soon they had church privileges in their new homes as they had had in their old ones. More, they were thus the means, under God, of the salvation of thousands upon thousands of immortal souls, many of which, in all human probability, never would have been saved otherwise. Mr. Paisley, who settled near Edwardsville, is a noted example. He had abundant opportunity to have gone into the "mother Church," under the specious plea now often made, that there is "little difference" between us; and, in so doing, might have gone into comparative obscurity. But he wrote an urgent letter to Rev. William Barnett, calling for help, and he gave it to Rev. Finis Ewing, who read it to his congregation in Kentucky, and they made up the means on the spot to furnish Mr. Barnett a horse to make the trip. He came, and although there was much opposition and misrepresentation from the "mother Church," yet they held a camp-meeting, at which at least *one* soul was converted, and a train of influences started which resulted in the organization of the old Bear Creek church, which is in successful operation to this day, having been the mother of not less than eight other flourshing congregations, which are still in existence, sustaining the means of grace, having neat and comfortable houses of worship, all out of debt, and a membership of four to five hundred, while hundreds, who have found Christ here, are in other lands, and hundreds more have gone up to join the church triumphant.

# CHAPTER III.

## SANGAMON PRESBYTERY.

REV. MR. BERRY—HIS LABORS—FIRST CONGREGATION ORGANIZED IN THE SANGAMON COUNTRY—OLD SUGAR CREEK—INTERESTING SCENE.

We have already seen that Rev. Mr. McLin settled in White county, in the southeastern part of the State, and that Rev. Mr. Rice settled in what was Madison, but now Bond county, and Rev. Mr. Berry went up into the interior of the State and settled near Springfield, the present capital. Thus these three preachers organized three nucleuses around which churches grew up, and an influence for good spread out in all directions. The first congregation organized in this upper country was, without much doubt, old Sugar Creek, which is still in working order, and has an active, intelligent membership. Its house of worship stands about ten miles south of the city of Springfield, and about five miles southeast of Chatham. It is in a rich and thriving community of farmers.

Just when Mr. Berry first settled is unknown to the writer, but we have already seen that Presbytery has met twice at old Sugar Creek, so that, in point of time, its organization was but little behind Hopewell and Bear Creek.

Mr. Knight says: "Rev. John M. Berry occupied the northern extremity of our operations in the State. He being an energetic and efficient minister, soon had quite a religious interest in that section of country. * * * * The Sangamon country was a very popular part of Illinois, and emigrants from Kentucky and other States were attracted there. * * * * But the attractions of the Sangamon country not only drew some of our people, but also some of our preachers from other States. Gilbert Dodds and Thomas Campbell from Kentucky, I believe, were the first. They were only licentiates when they came, and were both ordained by Illinois Presbytery."

The wisdom of the selection of this part of the State, by Mr. Berry and his compeers, as a home and field of labor, could not be called in question by any who have ever traveled over it. A more beautiful, fertile and well-improved country would be hard to find on the continent. And it must be a matter of gratitude to all true Cumberland Presbyterians, that in this grand country, where Messrs. Berry, Dodds, Campbell and others sowed the first seeds of the Church, Cumberland Presbyterians are strong and firmly rooted, having numerous churches well established, and the general interests of the church sustained, perhaps equal to any portion of our entire Church territory.

## SANGAMON PRESBYTERY.

Having given a sample of the doings of the first Presbytery organized, we pass on to introduce to the reader to the organization of the second Presbytery in the State. The Great Head of the Church had so blessed the labors of the fathers—Rev. Messrs. Berry, Dodds, Campbell and others—that several societies had been organized in Sangamon and adjacent counties, and several ministers were now wholly engaged within their bounds. The following is the order of Synod for the organization of this Presbytery:

"Sangamon Presbytery met agreeable to an order of Synod, (old Cumberland Synod,) viz: *Resolved*, That a Presbytery be stricken off the Illinois Presbytery, bounded as follows—beginning at the mouth of the Illinos river, thence up said river to the north line of town ten, thence with said line east to the little Wabash, thence down said stream to the south line of town seven, thence east with said line to the State line, thence north so as to include all the bounds north of the aforesaid lines, to be known by the name of Sangamon Presbytery; composed of the following members, viz: Rev. Messrs. David Foster, John M. Berry, Thomas Campbell, Gilbert Dodds and John Porter; to meet at the house of William Drennon, Sugar Creek, Sangamon county, State of Illinois, on the 20th of April, 1829, John M. Berry to be Modarator, and in case of his failure, Thomas Campbell.

"HIRAM A. HUNTER, *Moderator*.
"RICHARD BEARD, *Clerk*."

This **Moderator** and **Clerk** are both still living, and are as familiar to Cumberland Presbyterians as household words. The former resides in the city of Louisville, Kentucky, the latter in Lebanon, Tennessee. Father Drennon, at whose house this Presbytery met, was still living a few years ago, and the writer has more than once shared the hospitality of the family.

The record goes on: "Sangamon Presbytery was opened by a sermon delivered by the Rev. J. M. Berry, from Mark xvi. 15. Constituted by prayer. The above named members, appointed by Synod, were present, except John Porter, who was absent. Elder Joseph Dodds, representatives John Hamilton from Bethel, and Samuel Berry from Concord and Lebanon societies. John M. Berry, having been appointed by the last Synod first Moderator of this Presbytery, Gilbert Dodds was chosen Clerk. John M. Cameron, William McCord and Neill Johnson, licentiates, Payton Mitchell and Archibald Johnson, candidates, produced a regular dismission from the Illinois Presbytery, and they were therefore accordingly received. Needham Roach, a licentiate, formerly under care of the Nashville Presbytery, produced satisfactory testimony, and thereby was received under the care of this Presbytery. Payton Mitchell read a discourse from a text previously assigned him. Presbytery, after considering his case, thought proper not to continue him as a candidate. Thomas Campbell was chosen Stated Clerk for the Presbytery. Rev. David Foster was appointed the commissioner to the General Assembly, and furnished with suitable testimonials; and in case of his failure, Thomas Campbell. The societies of Concord and Lebanon were appointed to furnish an elder as commissioner to the General Assembly, and in case of their failure, Sugar Creek society one. Whereas, Thomas Campbell and the society of Spring Creek had previously entered into a contract (viz.:) that he was to preach one-half his time to them, and he giving satisfactory reasons to the Presbytery for wishing the contract dissolved, the Presbytery did, therefore, dissolve the contract. Gilbert Dodds and Sugar Creek society having previously entered into a contract (viz.: ) that he was to preach to them one-fourth of his time, for which they were to contribute something for his support, and they failing on their part, the Presbytery do, therefore, dissolve the said contract at his request.

"*Resolved*, That the Presbytery do hereby recommend to the ordained preachers that they attend to examinations in the different societies within their bounds, at least once a year.

"Whereas, It is impossible to supply the numerous calls in neighborhoods with preaching, from the cramped circumstances of ministers in the bounds of the Presbytery; *Resolved*, That it be and is hereby recommended to the societies and neighborhoods, destitute of preaching within the bounds of Sangamon Presbytery, that they unite and raise in each neighborhood or society, so destitute, such funds as they are able by voluntary contributions, place said funds in the hands of a suitable person, chosen by the neighborhood or society, to act as treasurer for them, whose duty it shall be to remunerate those preachers that may be sent by Presbytery to preach to them—say $1.00 per day. By this means the Presbytery can feel herself justifiable in sending such neighborhoods and societies as good supplies as may be in her power. Presbytery adjourned to meet at Lebanon meeting-house, Sangamon county, State of Illinois, on the second Tuesday of September next. Concluded with prayer.

"JOHN M. BERRY, *Moderator*.
"GILBERT DODDS, *Clerk*."

Thus we see the second Presbytery started on its way. The men who composed it are all gone to their reward. Of the licentiates present John M. Cameron and Neill Johnson only remain, both quite old, the former more than four-score years. Of the candidates, Archibald Johnson died in Kansas a few years since, and it is believed that Mr. Mitchell has been dead for many years.

Of the ministers who composed this Presbytery, Mr. Berry and Mr. Dodd are all with whom the writer formed any acquaintance. These latter continued to a good old age useful and worthy. Suitable sketches of their lives will be found in this volume in the proper place. The others had fallen at their posts and had gone to their rewards before my acquaintance in the State. It is to be greatly regretted that neither in this Presbytery, nor that of Illinois, do we find any list of the churches organized and under their care. It seems astonishing how such an important item was omitted. We see from the record that at the time of its organization, Sangamon Presbytery had at least five congregations under her care—Sugar Creek, Spring Creek, Concord, Lebanon and Bethel. Whether there were others it is impossible to tell from the record. All these, with possibly one exception, were in Sangamon county: for this county, at this period, covered an immense territory. It is worthy of note that all these societies are still in existence, with good houses of worship and the regular means of grace well sustained,

Thus, in six years, from three ministers, we find the little band had multiplied to nine, and are divided into two Presbyteries.

### PRESBYTERIAL MEETINGS.

We find the Fall Session of 1829 meeting at Lebanon, promptly. All the members present. Sermon by Mr. Berry. Neill Johnson was ordered to prepare for ordination at the next session. After some other routine business, adjourned to meet in the spring at Bethel meeting-house, in Morgan county. At this session Mr. Dodds was Moderator, and Mr. Campbell Clerk.

The Spring Session of 1830, on account of the church being repaired, was held at the house of Needham Roach. Sermon by Mr. Dodds. Four members present, one absent. The order for the ordination of Neill Johnson was extended until the next session. Archibald Johnson read a discourse from a text previously assigned him, which was not sustained, but another text was assigned.

The Fall Session of 1830 met September 29th, in the school-house near Robert Smith's, in Macon county. Sermon by Mr. Campbell. They adjourned to meet next day at Mt. Zion camp-ground; and here we first find the name of Andrew Wilson as representative from Mt. Zion congregation—a congregation which still stands as a noble monument of God's grace, from which a whole bevy of congregations have gone forth, she being the fruitful mother of nearly all the congregations now comprising Decatur Presbytery. Andrew Wilson will be recognized at once as the father of three Cumberland Presbyterian ministers—Rev. T. B. Wilson, D.D., late of Marshall, Texas; Rev. James Wilson, who died while at Cumberland College a few years ago; and Rev. A. M. Wilson, now of Fredonia, Kansas. Mr. Wilson, the father, had gone home to heaven before my acquaintance in the neighborhood, (1853,) but his worthy companion—"old Aunt Polly," as everybody called her—was living, and remained to a good old age, and went down to the grave as full of honors and the love of the people as she was full of years. Never have I known a more noble Christian mother than she. At this Presbytery Neill Johnson was ordained. He preached his trial sermon from I. Peter iii. 18. Mr. Campbell preached the ordination sermon and Mr. Foster presided and gave the charge. At this session, also, A. M. Wilson was received as a candidate for the ministry.

The Spring Session of 1831 was held in the schoolhouse in Concord congregation, April 7th. Sermon by Mr. Campbell. All the members present but Mr. Porter. Rev. James McDowell presented a letter from Logan Presbytery, and was thereby received as a member. The following *pungent* resolution passed by this session, we copy entire: "*Resolved*, That this Presbytery require the punctual attendance of each of her members at every subsequent meeting of Missouri Synod of the Cumberland Presbyterian Church; and each delinquent member shall render his excuse or excuses at the next meeting of Presbytery, and if his excuse or excuses are not judged providential, he shall be dealt with according to the magnitude of his offense, by rebuking and exhorting him to punctual attendance thereafter; and if such delinquent member or members shall continue negligent or obstinate, the Presbytery shall proceed to suspend or depose him or them as contumacious." From another resolution we learn that there were nine congregations on the roll, viz: Sugar Creek, Bethel, Spring Creek, Mackinaw, Jacksonville, Mount Zion, Lebanon, Mount Pleasant and Rock Creek. When these congregations were organized, or by whom, and when they were taken under the care of the Presbytery, the records show absolutely nothing. Illinois Presbytery had practiced this way, and the younger sister seems to love to walk in the ways of the older. We are reminded of the story of the boy who carried the stone in one end of the bag and the grain in the other, because his father had done so. At this session Archibald Johnson was licensed to preach.

The Fall Session of 1831 was held at Stout's Grove, in McLean county, Sept. 6th. Mr. Berry preached the opening sermon. Isaac Hill, a licentiate formerly under the care of Indiana Presbytery, and James M. Gladen, also a licentirte from Lebanon Presbytery, were received under the care of this Presbytery. John McCabe was received as a candidate for the ministry. We find the following, which shows very clearly how these brethren stood on these questions: "Ordered that each ordained and licentiate minister of this Presbytery use his influence to advance the interest of Sabbath-Schools, Bible, Tract and Temperance societies, and report at the next Presbytery.

We have followed the history of this young Presbytery, and find her growing stronger every session—stretching out her arms in all directions. We must now turn attention to the third Presbytery in the series, taking them in the order of their organization. Before leaving this Presbytery we wish to say, that we very much desired a more comprehensive and detailed statement of its history under the pen of the Stated Clerk, but failed to secure it. No Presbytery in the State has had more useful and prominent men connected with it; nor has any one acted a more conspicuous part in our Church affairs in Illinois. Identified with her history are the names of Berry, Campbell, Porter, Foster, the Johnsons, McDonells, Lansden, Reynolds, Dodds, Cameron, Potter, Haynes, the Lowrances, the Whites, the Bells, and many other noble men, who would be ornaments to any Church. We are happy to record that her present list of ministers are able and efficient men, and are doing a good work for Christ and mankind. In their proper place will be found sketches of several of her first ministers.

# CHAPTER IV.

### THE THIRD PRESBYTERY—VANDALIA.

The third Presbytery organized was Vandalia, of which the writer is at present a member. It was formed originally out of the southern part of Sangamon and the northern part of Illinois. To her territory belongs the ground where the first Presbytery in the State was organized. Old Bear Creek church is hers, and on her ground also lies sleeping the two Barbers, Foster, the two Knights, and Father McAdow.

The following succinct but very satisfactory and reliable historical synopsis of this Presbytery has been prepared by our present worthy Stated Clerk, Rev. W. W. M. Barber, esteemed pastor of the church at Windsor, Ill., which we are happy to give to our readers, *verbatim:*

"Vandalia Presbytery was constituted by order of Missouri Synod, October, 1831, while in session at New Lebanon church, Cooper county, Missouri. A resolution was passed, signed by Samuel King, as Moderator, and John R. Browne, Clerk, authorizing the formation of a Presbytery out of a part of Sangamon and a part of Illinois Presbyteries, to be known as *Vandalia Presbytery* of the C. P. Church. The name taken from what was then the capital of the State, and I suppose the largest town in the bounds of the Presbytery. In compliance with said resolution, on the first Tuesday in April, 1832, at the house of Rev. Joel Knight, in Montgomery county, Illinois, Revs. David Foster, John Barber, Sr., Joel Knight and John Barber, Jr., and Robert Paisley, a representative from Bear Creek congregation, met and constituted the Presbytery, Rev. David Foster acting as Moderator by appointment of Synod, who was also *elected* Moderator, and John Barber, Jr., was elected Clerk, and he was also elected Stated Clerk. John Knight, A. F. Trousdale, Wm. Finley, Joseph Howard and Isaac Hill were licentiates, and Mathew Gillespie, Samuel Parr and John McKabe were candidates, under the care of the Presbytery at her first session.

"There is no record of the congregations at the first, nor several of the following meetings, so we are left without that valuable part of our history. The meeting was then composed, so far as we can gather from the records, of four ordained ministers, one representative, five licentiates and three candidates. Rev. David Foster was the first commissioner to the General Assembly, with John Barber, Sr., as alternate, and William Young, of New Lebanon, on the part of the eldership, with Mathew Gillespie, of Mt. Pisgah, as alternate. At the first session, Isaac Baird was received as a candidate for the ministry. Some resolutions were passed upon the subject of education, thus identifying Vandalia Presbytery, in her incipiency, with the great subject of education, and also agreeing to co-operate with the American Sunday-school Union.

"The second meeting was at the house of Hugh Watson, Bond county, October, 1832. All the ordained ministers were present. There is no record showing that the candidates and licentiates were present, but during the business William Finley, John Knight and Isaac Hill were ordered to prepare for ordination at next meeting. There were present as representatives from congregations: James Law, Mt. Zion, Michael Walker, Bear Creek, William Young, New Lebanon, and Henry S. Grove, Big Creek. Since the constitution, this Presbytery has held (1876) about ninety-five sessions. There are records of ninety in the hands of the Stated Clerk, and it is supposed that there are five missing records. Some of these meetings have been called, or special meetings. In the forty-four years of the Presbytery's existence, there has been but two or three failures to meet on adjournment.

"The bounds are not so large as when first organized, and I am not prepared to give the boundary lines. Other Presbyteries have portions of territory that once belonged to Vandalia. There were three candidates under the care of Presbytery at the beginning; there have been fifty-seven received since, making sixty in all. The following named persons are reported to have been received as candidates for the ministry since the first: Isaac Baird, Joseph Barlow, James Ashmore, E. Alexander, J. M. Bone, Ministre Jones, Joseph Gorden, John W. Woods, Levi Beals, Edwin Owens, Robert Hill, A. M. Wilson, E. Canaday, A. N. Ashmore, Thomas M. Davis, T. M. Finley, W. B. Rice, T. K. Hedges, Thomas Gwinn, William Blizzard, Jefferson Fruit, T. A. Bone, W. C. Harris, J. S. Freeland, James M. Wooseley, A. W. Smith, C. G. Keown, E. R. Rodgers, J. C. Crowder, J. M. Lackey, A. Keown, E. S. Carr, C. T. Linxwiler, W. W. M. Barber, W. L. Bankson, J. A. Slaughter, J. B. Hunter, W. B. Poland, Isaac Chapman, J. A. Foulks, R. B. Crossman, T. W. McDavid, D. H. Starkey, A. W. Hawkins, G. F. Berry, S. F. Minor, A. B. McDavid, Lafayette Starkey, Bruce Buley W. J. McDavid, F. H. Culley, A. C. Biddle, I. N. Pettijohn, R. H. McHenry, G. L. Hunter. Of this number twenty-two have been discontinued as candidates; two are reported as having died, viz., Ministre Jones and E. S. Carr; two have been dismissed by letter, viz., J. B. Hunter, who entered the ministry in the U. B. Church, and A. W. Hawkins, missionary (1876) at Logansport, Indiana. It is likely that some of the brethren have been stricken off by action of Synod in the change of Presbyterial lines, or have been transferred in some other way, as some are in the ministry who have been received as candidates by Vandalia Presbytery, of whom the records give no account, or it may be the missing records give the account.

"There have been, according to record, twenty-two licensures performed, and the reception of eleven from other Presbyteries and other denominations. The following are the names of those licensed by the Presbytery: Joseph Barlow, James Ashmore, J. M. Bone, Joseph Gorden, John W. Woods, A. M. Williams, T. A. Bone, C. G. Keown, E. R. Rodgers, A. Keown, C. T. Linxwiler, W. W. M. Barber, W. L. Bankson, W B. Poland, T. W. McDavid, D. H. Starkey, S. F. Minor, A. B. McDavid, W. J. McDavid, F. H. Culley, G. L. Hunter, R. H. McHenry. Those received as licentiates: Cyrus Haynes, Ben. Smith, T. K. Hedges, S. Y. Anderson, R. Knoll, Geo. O'Bannon, S. H. Haire, A. Ripetoe, X. G. McDowell, A. J. Huffman, C. L. McLain. These all make thirty-three licentiates having been under the care of the Presbytery. There may have been more, as the record is defective. Of these, the licensure of the five following named have been revoked, viz: A. Keown, S. Y. Anderson, S. H. Haire, S. F. Minor, A. J. Huffman; and the license of A. F. Trousdale, after a long conflict, was also revoked. Six licentiates have been dismissed regularly, either by letter or by change of Presbyterial lines, viz: J. W. Woods, A. W. Smith, C. G. Keown, X. G. McDowell, D. H. Starkey, C. L. McLain.

"There have been twenty-five ordinations by the Presbytery, viz: John Knight, Wm. Finley, Isaac Hill, J. Barlow, James Ashmore, J. M. Bone, Joseph Gorden, C. Haynes, A. M. Wilson, Ben. A. Smith, T. K. Hedges, T. A. Bone, E. R. Rodgers. R. Knoll, W. W. M. Barker, C. T. Linxwiler, W. L. Bankson, W. B. Poland, A. Rippetoe, Geo. O'Bannan, T. W. McDavid, F. H. Culley, A. B. McDavid, W. J. McDavid, G. L. Hunter; and there have been thirty-five ordained ministers received, viz: David Campbell, Neill Johnson, Daniel Traughber, S. McAdow, (by resolution,

October 4th, 1838,) N. Carper, (colored,) T. W. B. Dawson.
J. S. Freeland, W. T. Hutchison, C. G. Keown, T. H.
Hardwick, S. W. Goodnight, J. B. Logan, W. W. Brown,
John Bennet, W. Turner, R. J. P. Lemmon, G. W. Montgomery, A. Finley, A. Johnson, W. P. Baker, L. P. Deatherage,
(three times, twice by letter and once by action of Central
Illinois Synod,) C. Y. Hudson, A. F. Hutchison, E. Canaday,
J. C. Hamilton, J, R. Brown, D. R. Bell, J. M. Galloway, S.
B. Redman, J. W. Blosser, (twice,) H. Melville J. T. May, J.
H. Hendrick, E. B. Crisman, R. J. Beard; which number
added to those ordained by Presbytery, and the four original
members, would make sixty-four ordained ministers who have
had a connection with the Presbytery. Of this number, one
(T. W. B. Dawson) has been solemnly deposed from the
ministry, who, I think, entered the ministry in the Baptist
denomination. Five have been dropped from the roll, viz:
R. Knoll, who was received from the Lutheran church and
returned to the same; Joseph Barlow, who was for a while
suspended, then restored, and finally discontinued as a
minister—he is now dead; E. Canaday was received on a
letter from the Rushville Presbytery, and afterward his name
was dropped from the roll of ordained ministers, at his
request—where he is or what he is doing I do not know; F.
H. Culley, who is now suspended from the ministry; and S.
B. Redman, having entered the United Brethren church
before asking a dismission from Presbytery, his name was
stricken from the roll. Thirty have been regularly dismissed,
either by letter or change of Presbyterial lines. Twelve have
died, the first of which was Rev. David Foster, who died
and was buried near Silver creek, Madison county, in the
bounds of the Presbytery, and upon his tomb is the following
inscription: 'In memory of the Rev. David Foster, who was
born May 4th, 1780, joined Presbytery in 1804, was licensed
in 1805, was ordained in 1810, and died May 9th, 1833, aged
53 years and 5 days. *He was a good man.—Acts xi. 24.*'

"On the 14th of June, 1833, the Presbytery met in regular session, and on the 15th passed the following resolutions:

"WHEREAS, It has pleased the Great Head of the Church to remove, by death, the Rev. David Foster from the councils and labors of this Presbytery;

"*Resolved*, That she feels deeply afflicted at the loss occasioned by his death.

"*Resolved*, That this Presbytery cherish, with unfeigned respect, the memory of the Rev. David Foster; and

"*Resolved*, Further, that the Stated Clerk of the Presbytery forward for publication in the *Revivalist* a copy of the foregoing preamble and resolutions, together with an account of the life of the Rev. David Foster, so far as he may be able to collect facts on that subject.

"The second minister that died was Rev. John Barber, Jr., and upon the records of the Presbytery in October 4th, 1838, we find the following: 'The Presbytery would desire to feel submissive to the dispensation of divine providence, while with strange sensation she records her inexpressable loss in the removal of one of her beloved members by death, namely, Bro. John Barber, Jr., who departed this life on the 22d day of April, 1838.' His remains are buried in Madison county, south of Edwardsville.

"The third that died was Rev. N. Carper, (colored,) and upon the records of October 2d, 1840, we have this:

"WHEREAS, It has pleased the Great Head of the Church to remove Bro. Nicholas Carper by death, from his earthly labors, Presbytery would hereby express her high sense of the moral worth of Bro. Carper and the loss she has sustained in the removal of such an esteemed fellow-laborer.

"The fourth that died was old Father McAdow, and in regard to his death, we have the following: 'It has been the privilege of this Presbytery, for a number of years past, to have the name of Samuel McAdow, one of their fathers, which first organized the Cumberland Presbyterian Church, enrolled among her ministers, and although he had been laid aside, by infirmity, from active labors for a time, yet, in his meekness, humility and other personal virtues, as also his agreeable manners, his instructive counsels, his ardent, unaffected piety, had endeared him to us all, who knew him personally; not only as one of the Fathers of the Church, but also a great support to the Church'; and,

"WHEREAS, It has pleased the sovereign disposer of all events to remove said Father McAdow on the 30th of March, 1841, from the scenes of his toils and labors below to his rest above, and as the name of McAdow must be embalmed in every heart of all real Cumberland Presbyterians—to the members of Vandalia Presbytery is that name particularly dear, and his removal is felt as a severe loss, and the chasm there made will doubtless continue long unfilled.

"*Resolved*, Therefore, that this Presbytery hereby expresses her high sense of Father McAdow's real worth, and deeply sympathizes with the bereaved friends of the deceased, and appoint that a funeral sermon be preached on the occasion (to-morrow) by Bro. John Barber, a member of this Presbytery.

"He is buried at Mt. Gilead, Bond county, Illinois. The above action was had by Presbytery at Mt. Gilead, April 6th, 1844.

"There is something a little peculiar in the reception of Father McAdow, to which I wish to call attention. The record is found in the minutes of October, 1838.

"WHEREAS, Father McAdow is living in the bounds of Vandalia Presbytery, and has not, for a number of years, been noticed on her records, nor on any other records of the church; and,

"WHEREAS, It is truly desirable that he should not go out of notice, but that he should be kept in view, so that his name and his character may be properly appreciated, and his death, when it shall take place, duly and officially recorded.

"*Resolved*, Therefore, that his name be placed on the records of this Presbytery as a member, who is always to be present or absent at discretion.

"The fifth minister, belonging to the Presbytery, that died, was Rev. T. A. Bone; but as the records of the Presbytery are lost from the fall of 1852 to the fall of 1853—two sessions missing here—the record of his death does not appear on the minutes. He is buried at Marrowbone, Illinois.

"The sixth minister that died was Rev. John Barber, Sr., who died September 19th, 1855. On the record of the Presbytery, while in session at Union Grove, Bond county, Illinois, April 25th, 1856, the following was adopted:

"WHEREAS, It has pleased Almighty God to remove from our midst, since the last session of the Presbytery, Rev. John Barber, the oldest and one of the most zealous, active, devoted and efficient ministers of this Presbytery—a man universally beloved for his public and private virtues, and one of the pioneers of the C. P. Church in Southern Illinois; therefore,

"*Resolved*, That while we bow with submission to this afflictive dispensation of Divine providence, we would recognize the warning voice of God to be also ready to render up our account with joy and not with regret.

"*Resolved*, That we sincerely lament the loss of Father Barber, not only as a pastor and evangelist, but also in the councils of the Church.

"*Resolved*, That we sincerely sympathize with his bereaved family, numerous friends and the whole Church in this Presbytery, in this sad bereavement.

"*Resolved*, That as a suitable testimony of our esteem for his memory, that Rev. Joel Knight be requested to preach his funeral on nexth Sabbath, at 11 o'clock, at this place.

"*Resolved*, That we will strive, as a Presbytery, to emulate his high example in his self-sacrificing labors to win souls to Christ, and to build up the Redeemer's kingdom—and like him endeavor to die at our post.

"*Resolved*, That a copy of this preamble and resolutions be presented to the family of the deceased, and also a copy be sent to the *Missouri Cumberland Presbyterian* for publication.

"He was buried at old Bear Creek, Montgomery county, Illinois.

"The seventh minister that died was Rev. J. S. Freeland, and on the fall minutes, October 20th, 1856, is the following:

"WHEREAS, It has pleased the Great Head of the Church to call from his labors on earth to his reward in heaven, our beloved brother and fellow-laborer, Rev. J. S. Freeland, during our last session of Presbytery; therefore,

"*Resolved*, That we feel greatly afflicted and stricken under this sore bereavement, being called suddenly to part with one in the bloom of youth and in the midst of great usefulness.

"*Resolved*, That we, as ministers and people, feel solemnly admonished by this dispensation of divine providence, to live more faithful and devoted to our work, that we may be found standing at our post when the messenger comes.

"*Resolved*, That we deeply sympathize with his bereaved family, his afflicted congregations to whom he preached, and also with the pupils and friends of Sullivan Academy, over which he has presided with such acceptance, in this sudden bereavement.

"*Resolved*, That a copy of these resolutions be presented to the widow of the deceased, and the *Missouri Cumberland Presbyterian* for publication, and that a committee be appointed to prepare a suitable obituary of the deceased for publication in the church papers.

"He is buried at Marrowbone, Illinois.

"The eighth minister that died was Rev. John Knight, and on the minutes of the session of October 3d, 1859, we have the following:

"WHEREAS, Almighty God, in his allwise providence, has removed from our midst, by death, since our last session, from his labors on earth to his reward on high, Rev. John

Knight, one of our oldest and most experienced members; therefore,

"*Resolved*, That in the death of Bro. Knight, the Presbytery has lost one of its most exemplary and devoted members, a safe and wise counsellor, and the Church a zealous, spiritual and able minister of the gospel.

"*Resolved*, That we will endeavor to imitate his example of humility and devotedness to the service of God, and his self-sacrificing spirit.

"*Resolved*, That we deeply sympathize with the aged widow and bereaved family, also with the Union congregation.

"He is buried in Fayette county, Illinois.

"The ninth minister that died was Rev. W. T. Hutchison, and on the records of Presbytery, at her session at Bethalto, March, 1868, we have the following:

"*Resolved*, 1st. That in the death of Bro. Hutchison, this Presbytery has lost one of her oldest ministers, one who was a safe counsellor and a useful preacher, an affectionate father and husband, and citizen—beloved by all who knew him.

"2d. That we view, in this providence of God, a loud warning to all the remaining members of this body, 'to be up and doing while it is day, for the time is at hand when no man can work longer.'

"3d. That Rev. J. M. Bone be requested to prepare a suitable obituary for publication, embodying the most prominent events connected with his life, and that his funeral be preached at the next regular session of this Presbytery, by some one appointed by the Moderator.

"4th. That having been assured 'that his name is entered in the Lamb's book of life, and he has entered into the full enjoyment of fellowship of the saints in light,' that his name, therefore, be discontinued on the roll.

"Rev. Joel Knight preached his funeral at the next session of the Presbytery. He is buried at Union Grove, Bond county, Illinois.

"The tenth and eleventh ministers that died were Revs. A. Finley and W. B. Poland, and on the records of Presbytery while in session at Windsor, April, 1870, we have the following action:

"We feel that in the death of these brethren, especially Bro. Poland, our Heavenly Father has sent us an admonition that we should heed as a Presbytery, 'that our time is short and uncertain, and what we do in the great vineyard of the Master must be done quickly;' therefore,

"*Resolved*, That in the loss of these beloved ministers this Presbytery recognizes the voice of the Great Head of the Church, calling us to greater diligence, humility and consecration to our work, 'for the night cometh when no man can work.'

"*Resolved*, That in the death of these, especially in that of Bro. Poland, cut down as it were in the midst of usefulness, this Presbytery has lost worthy laborers and counsellors, and the congregations to whom they ministered have lost successful under-shepherds.

"*Resolved*, That we, as a Presbytery, do deeply sympathize with the bereaved congregations and relatives of the deceased, and pray that the Great Head of the Church may overrule this deep affliction for the good of Presbytery and the glory of his name.

"Rev. A. Finley is buried at Mt. Pleasant, and W. B. Poland at McDavid's Point. Both places are in Montgomery county, Illinois.

"The twelfth minister that died was Rev. Joel Knight, and on the minutes of Presbytery, in session March 27th, 1876, Sullivan, Illinois, we have the following:

"Rev. Joel Knight, the oldest member of this Presbytery, and one of the oldest ministers, at his death, in our denomination, departed this life at his residence in Donnellson, Illinois, February 2d, 1876, wanting 20 days of being 80 years of age.

"*Resolved*, That in the departure of Father Knight, this

Presbytery has lost a safe and wise counsellor, his family a kind husband and father, the country a worthy citizen, and the Church at large a faithful and efficient minister of the gospel for more than fifty years.

"*Resolved 2d*, That in the character of Father Knight, we have an example of diligence in the discharge of duty, punctuality in all his engagements, and a long life which are unblemished and consecrated, worthy of our highest emulation, and is a treasure left to the Church far more precious than gold and rubies.

"*Resolved 3d*, That we deeply sympathize with his bereaved wife, children, and relatives, and the entire Church, in this bereavement, and we will receive his sudden and unexpected departure as an admonition to us all, 'to be fathful to our vows, and to stand with our loins girt about and our lamps burning and ready for the coming of the bridegroom.'

"*Resolved 4th*, That in memory of the worth of our departed father in Israel, his funeral be preached at next meeting of Presbytery, and that a copy of this action be given to the widow of the deceased, also that it be published in the papers of the Church.

"Rev. J. B. Logan preached his funeral. He is buried near Old Union, Montgomery county, Illinois.

"There are now sixteen ordained ministers belonging to the Presbytery, and one licentiate. Of the congregations I cannot speak definitely. There are, according to my information, the names of fifty-three—some names have been changed, and are counted twice. The following are the names: Bear Creek, New Lebanon, Mt. Pisgah, Mt. Zion, Big Creek, Mt. Carmel, Bethany, Beaver Creek, Mt. Gilead, Silver Creek, Smyrna, Hickory Creek, South Fork, Good Prospect, Union, Locust Grove, Zion, New Salem, New Providence, Shiloh, Columbia, Goshen, Brushy Hill, Antioch, Pleasant Prairie, Omphghent, East Fork, Taylorville, Sullivan, Lake Fork, Pleasant Grove, Mt. Pleasant, Union Grove,

Alton, Hurricane, Windsor, McDavid's Point, Mt. Tabor, Irving, Maple Grove, Walshville, Bethalto, Friendship, Audubon, Hillsboro, Palmer, Morrisonville, Upper Alton, Union, American Bottom, Pleasant Mound, New Hope, Witt and Mattoon. Some are extinct, others are in the bounds of other Presbyteries, so that there are but twenty-two now on the roll."

### REFLECTIONS.

I will add a few words of my own. In the Spring of 1854, I first visited this Presbytery. It was then in session with old Bear Creek Church. The Presbytery was held in a school-house, the old church being occupied with preaching. It was a frame, with split boards nailed on as weather-boarding. It would seat, perhaps, 150 persons. This was nearly as good a church-house as was in the bounds any where. There were not more than five or six houses of worship—all of this quality, or no better—in the Presbytery. All told they were not worth $10,000—perhaps not the half of that sum. There were at this session, the two Knights, Hutchison, Barlow, Barber, Sr., Wilson, J. M. Bone, Hodges, Freelin and Hardwick. I was a visitor. Great harmony prevailed. But I was much impressed with the labor done and pay received. All these ministers did not receive $500 per annum for their services, and now that the field had been occupied, after a fashion, for thirty years, very little had been done of a *permanent* character. There was not a self-sustaining congregation in the Presbytery. I do not remember that there was in the entire State. By self-sustaining, I mean one that sustained the means of grace regularly in their midst. All these preachers had to depend upon their own physical or mental labor, outside the ministry, for a part of their support. These were devoted, but poor men, and had to struggle against fearful difficulties to preach at all; but they preached on as best they could, and God was with them. One reason why churches were not permanent, was the fluctuating nature of society. People were moving here and there, and permanent no where, The country, as already stated, was regarded as very sickly, and many who came out from the older states, would get discouraged and go back, or move some where else. Congregations did not increase in numbers much—indeed it was hard work to hold their own. These congregations, with perhaps two exceptions, were all in the country. But a better day soon began to dawn upon us. Railroads entered and crossed the state in all directions; enterprise started up as by magic everywhere; leagues of unimproved lands were bought up and became valuable; towns and cities began to grow; where before had been nought but the howling wilderness, now the entire country is inclosed in cultivated farms or in pastures. The health has greatly improved, society become settled, and Illinois has become the great "Prairie State," only third in the Union in point of resources, while our young Presbytery has lengthened her cords and strengthened her stakes, until she has twenty good church-houses, twelve of them being in towns or villages, and these houses are estimated at $67,860 in the statistical table of the General Assembly for 1877.

All these ministers named are gone to heaven, except two, Revs. J. M. Bone and A. M. Wilson, who are laboring in the State of Kansas. The churches still continue to sustain an annual drain by an immense emigration to the farther west, but still our numbers are not diminished but gradually increased. The same table puts down the amount paid last year, to pastors and supplies, at $4,542—full nine times the amount received twenty-four years ago. We have at least *eight* ministers who are wholly consecrated to their work, and follow no secular calling. The full statistics will be found in their proper place. Meanwhile we record this great advance with profound gratitude to God, especially as this is the ground first largely occupied by Cumberland Presbyterians, and where the first Presbytery in the State was organized.

# CHAPTER V.

### ORGANIZATION OF THE FIRST SYNOD.

Having given a brief history of the organization of the first three Presbyteries in the State, we come now to notice the organization of the first Synod. From a small handfull the Church has grown and multiplied until she has become a power in the land. At the General Assembly at Nashville, Tennessee, May 17th, 1832, the following was passed:

"*Resolved*, That a new Synod be constituted consisting of the following Presbyteries—Illinois, Sangamon, St. Louis and Vandalia, (now belonging to the Missouri Synod,) to be called the Illinois Synod; and that the first meeting be held at Mount Gilead meeting-house, Bond county, Illinois, on the second Thursday in October, 1832, and that the Rev. David Foster be the first Moderator, and in case of his absence, the Rev. David McLin.

"SAMUEL KING, *Moderator*.

"A copy test: Wm. H. Bingham, *Clerk*."

The Synod met according to this appointment, at Mount Gilead church. Sermon by Mr. Foster from Mark xvi. 20. Mr. Foster was elected Moderator, and John R. Browne, Clerk.

Members present: From Illinois Presbytery, Revs. D. W. McLin and Jas. S. Alexander; from Sangamon Presbytery, Revs. Gilbert Dodds, James McDowell and Thos. Campbell; from Vandalia Presbytery, Revs. David Foster, Joel Knight, John Barber, Sr., and John Barber, Jr.; from St. Louis Presbytery, Revs. Frank M. Braly, John Linville, Robert

Rennick and John R. Browne. Absentees: There were two from Illinois Presbytery, from Sangamon Presbytery three, from St. Louis Presbytery three.

There were elders present: From Illinois Presbytery, Lawrence Rollefson; from Vandalia Presbytery, James Low, Lewis Kear, James Johnston and Robert W. Denny; from Sangamon Presbytery, John Hamilton; from St. Louis Presbytery, Dr. John Young, Benjamin Bennett, James Kincaid and George W. Rennick.

Ministers thirteen, and elders ten, making a Synod of twenty-three in all. This ought to shame our present Synodical meetings, for many times we do not have this number now, when there are *four times* the number of ministers and churches to be represented in Synod. The report on the State of Religion at this meeting, was in substance, that within the last year there had been "4 congregations organized, adult baptisms 86, infant baptisms 102, professions of religion 443, accessions 219. The temperance cause and Sunday-schools are prospering, and the opposition to them is giving way among the people under your influence. Harmony and brotherly love seem to abound among your churches generally." We submit if that is not an encouraging report, under the circumstances. We take great pleasure in quoting, *verbatim*, the following action of this first Synod. It shows the animus of the people represented there:

### SUNDAY-SCHOOLS.

"*Resolved*, Unanimously, as the opinion of this Synod, that Sabbath-schools are an excellent means for the religious instruction and salvation of the rising generation, and as especially adapted to the necessities of the Valley of the Mississippi; and further, that this Synod approve of the 'American Sunday-school Union' as a great concentration of benevolent wisdom and energy for the accomplishment of the work of Sabbath-schools, and this Synod hereby recommends the general measures of that Union, while conducted on the broad and liberal principles which have hitherto distinguished their progress, to the ardent prayers and active co-operation of the different churches under her care."

#### OTHER BENEVOLENT OBJECTS.

They further recommended to the Presbyteries and churches under their care, "that they use all diligence in promoting and encouraging the establishment of Bible, Tract and Temperance societies within the sphere of their influence, as a means in the hand of God, of christianizing, and as a consequence of moralizing, the human family."—Minutes pp. 4, 5.

Thus we see how the denomination stood on these great questions, of the Bible Society, Tract Society, Sunday-schools and Temperance, when taking their ecclesiastical position before the world *forty years ago*. No denomination of Christians in the land have been more uniform and positive in their testimony on these questions than have Cumberland Presbyterians.

The second session of Synod was held at Pisgah meeting-house, St. Louis county, Missouri, October, 17th, 1833. Prior to this meeting Rev. David Foster, the Moderator, had been called to his final home. A sketch of his life will be found at the proper place in this work. He was in the State about six years, but he did a great and good work before he fell. Rev. John M. Berry preached the opening sermon from Acts xx. 28. Ministers present: John M. Berry, John Barber, Sr., John Barber, Jr., Joel Knight, William Finley, Robert Rennick, John Linville, John R. Browne, Jacob Clark, Frank M. Braly, John H. Garvin. Rev. John Barber, Sr., was Moderator, and Frank M Braly, Clerk.

As an evidence of the divine approval upon their work, we quote from their report on the state of religion, that during the past year there had been in the bounds of the Synod, and under the ministrations of her ministers, "760 conversions, 147 adult baptisms, 119 infant baptisms, accessions to the Church 324, and one Presbytery (Illinois) did not report her accessions and four new congregations."

### RUSHVILLE PRESBYTERY.

At the meeting of Synod in Sugar Creek church, Sangamon county, Illinois, October 21st, 1835, we find the following action recorded—minutes, pp. 16, 17:

"*Resolved*, That a Presbytery be stricken off the Sangamon Presbytery, to be composed of the following ministers, John M. Berry, Benjamin Conley, James M. Stockton and Cyrus Haynes, to be known by the name of *Rushville Presbytery*—then comes the boundaries, which we deem not important to insert—said Presbytery to hold its first meeting at Rushville, on the second Thursday in March, 1836, John M. Berry to be its first Moderator, and in case of his failure, Benjamin Conley."

At this meeting of Synod, Rev. Neill Johnson was Moderator, and Cyrus Haynes Clerk. Thus the fourth Presbytery comes into being, and is started on its way to do good. It is scarcely needful to say that it is still in existence, doing good work for the Master: being, perhaps, better manned with able and efficient ministers, than at any former period.

### MACKINAW PRESBYTERY.

Just one year from the passage of the order originating Rushville Presbytery, we find the Synod in session at Rushville, Illinois, October 20th, 1836, at which time and place the following resolution prevailed—Minutes p. 19:

"*Resolved*, That a new Presbytery be stricken from Sangamon Presbytery, to be composed of the following members, Neill Johnson, James McDowell, James E. Davis and Archibald Johnson. \* \* \* \* That Neill Johnson be the first Moderater, and in case of his failure, James McDowell.

Thus the fifth daughter came into being, *nameless* so far as the record is concerned. It is recorded on the next session of the Synod as Mackinaw Presbytery, and its being not thus recorded in the resolution we suppose to be an omission in the transcribing clerk.

#### FOSTER PRESBYTERY.

At the meeting of the Synod at Mount Carmel meeting-house, Montgomery county, Illinois, October 12th, 1837, Foster Presbytery was originated by the following action, found on minutes, page 22.

"On motion, resolved that a new Presbytery, to be known by the name of Foster Presbytery, be stricken off from Vandalia Presbytery, \* \* \* \* to be constituted by the following members, Brothers Isaac Hill, David Campbell and James Ashmore; and that Brother William Finley be attached to said Presbytery until such time as she shall have strength to do without him; and that all the licentiates and candidates, in said bounds, be under the care of said Presbytery, and that said Presbytery hold its first session on Thursday before the first Sabbath in April, 1838, in Charleston, Coles county, Illinois; and that Brother William Finley be the first Moderator, and in case of his absence, Brother Isaac Hill."

After the meeting of Synod in 1834, we find no more record of St. Louis Presbytery, and we presume she had been stricken off by the action of the Assembly, in 1835, and joined to Missouri Synod. At the meeting of the General Assembly, in 1838, Sangamon Synod was organized by striking off Rushville, Sangamon and Mackinaw Presbyteries, leaving Illinois, Vandalia and Foster comprising the Synod of Illinois.

# CHAPTER VI.

### SANGAMON SYNOD.

This was the second Synod founded in the State. The population, especially in the middle and more northern counties, had rapidly increased, and the distance over which members of Synod had to travel from the extreme bounds of their territory, was such that it was deemed advisable to ask the General Assembly to divide Illinois Synod, and organize a new Synod out of the northern part of her territory. The Stated Clerk, Rev. W. S. Campbell, D.D., has kindly furnished us the following copy of the organization of the new Synod, which will tell its own story:

"Sangamon (alias Mehaca) Synod of the Cumberland Presbyterian Church, met in Rushville, Illinois, October 18th, 1838, agreeably to the order of the General Assembly requiring its constitution. Brother John M. Berry, being present, presided. The Synod was constituted by prayer. The following members were present: From Sangamon Presbytery, John M. Berry, Thomas Campbell, with his elder, Richard Matthews; absent, Gilbert Dodds, Benjamin Conley, Abner W. Lansden and George W. Reynolds. From Rushville Presbytery, Abner McDowell, with his elder Micaiah Warren; Peter Downey, with his elder Joel Hargrove; Cyrus Haynes, with his elder John L. Ewing: absent, Samuel B. F. Caldwell and James M. Stockton. From Mackinaw Presbytery, James McDowell, with his elder Archy Bryant; James E. Davis, with his elder John Dickey: absent, Neill Johnson, Archibald Johnson and R. D. Taylor.

Bro. John Berry was chosen Moderator, and Cyrus Haymes Clerk.

"On motion, the Synod proceeded to the election of Stated Clerk, whereupon Cyrus Haynes was chosen Stated Clerk of this Synod."

It will thus be seen that this Synod has been in existence thirty-nine years. It was constituted with thirteen members present, six of them elders. It occupies about the same territory still, and comprises the same Presbyteries she did then. There is no finer farming country on the globe, perhaps, than is occupied by this Synod. For ten or fifteen years after its organization, the churches in this Synod seemed to gain more rapidly in numbers than did those of the Synod of Illinois. But after the slavery question began to be a constant bone of contention, the emigration from the older parts of the Church ceased almost entirely to come to Illinois, and turned into Missouri, Arkansas and Texas. What did come into this State, lodged, for the most part, in the counties more southern; and the membership, being yearly decreased by many removals and deaths, Sangamon Synod for another period of ten or fifteen years did not gain much in membership. But since the close of the war and the amicable settlement of the questions connected with it, and especially since the establishment and successful operation of Lincoln University, which is within the bounds of this Synod, the churches have advanced in membership and all the elements of progress. Indeed, in the darkest period of the Church, in this Synod, even when small progress was being made in additions to the membership, there was substantial progress all the time, in building church-houses, neat and comfortable. Cumberland Presbyterians have church-houses in the following towns among others: Girard, Auburn, Lincoln, Atlanta, Gibson, Tallula, Greenview, Virginia, LeRoy, Abingdon, and others not remembered.

It will be seen that this Synod had, at its organization, only sixteen ministers, all told. All of these have gone to their long homes but two, Rev. Neill Johnson, of McMinnville, Oregon, and Rev. Geo. W. Reynolds, of Carrollton, Illinois. These brethren are both "old and well stricken in years," and will soon join their fellow-laborers on the other happy shore. This Synod has now on its roll *fifty-three* ordained ministers and eleven probationers. The county which contains the largest number of churches and members is Menard. It is doubtful whether any denomination has a stronger hold in this county than Cumberland Presbyterians.

In this Synod, as well as the other two, it is to be regretted that a portion of the ministry are almost wholly *secularized*. They have their farms and cultivate them as other people do, therefore the churches are not well trained under their ministry; and, in our judgment, never can be trained to regular systematic work, while the chief time of the pastor or supply is engaged with his own secular affairs. We are met with the oft repeated reply, "that the churches do not sustain the ministry, and this secular work is a *necessity*." We are not sure of this. It was necessity thirty years ago, but we do not believe there is any necessity now for a secularized ministry in as old and well-furnished country as Illinois. After a country gets able to support the gospel, for ministers to keep on supporting themselves on the farm, is like a man keeping on with his torch-light after the sun has risen. The time is upon us when this way of living ought not to be tolerated by the Presbyteries in the old and established portions of the Church. No Church can advance and make progress with such a ministry, however talented, and learned, and able otherwise they may be. Their time, attention and abilities must be given to the Church and not to their farms. A *consecrated* ministry is what we, as a Church, need above all other things. If all the one hundred and thirty-three ordained ministers, now in the State, were every day devoted to the work of the ministry, our numbers would be doubled in three years or less, and perhaps our financial resources also. The churches are much to blame, we know, but all of the censure does not belong to them. There are ministers among us who have never thrown themselves on the Church for a year and *tested* the matter of a support. They really do not know whether they can be sustained of the gospel or not. But progress has been made, even in this matter, and we expect greater advancement still.

### ·DECATUR PRESBYTERY.

We are very glad to submit to the reader the following interesting summary of the organization and work of this Presbytery from the pen of the Stated Clerk, Rev. N. M. Baker. It is full and interesting, and will supercede much being added by the writer.

" At a meeting of the Sangamon Synod of the Cumberland Presbyterian Church, October, 1858, the following resolution was adopted:

" WHEREAS, Certain ministers and churches in the bounds of Sangamon and Mackinaw Presbyteries, collectively and mutually pray that Sangamon Synod cut off all that part of Sangamon Presbytery being and lying north and east of the south fork of Sangamon River; thence from the mouth of the Sangamon River to the rock ford of Salt Creek; thence with said creek to the third principal meridian; thence to the northwest corner of Macon county; thence east to the Foster Presbytery; thence with the line of Illinois Synod to the place of beginning; and constitute the same as a Presbytery to be known as the Decatur Presbytery of the Cumberland Presbyterian Church. Therefore,

"*Resolved,* That this Synod grant the prayer of said ministers and churches, and that the ordained ministers, viz: D. Traughber, J. C. Smith, J. B. Lowrance, G. W. Kinsolving and John Bennett, together with all the licentiates, candidates and churches under their care in said bounds be and they are hereby constituted a Presbytery, to be known as the Decatur Presbytery of the Cumberland Presbyterian Church, to hold its first session at Mt. Zion, Macon county, Ill., on Thursday next preceding the second Sabbath in April, A. D. 1859, at 7 o'clock P. M., and that Rev. D. Traughber be the first Moderator, or in case of his absence, that the Rev. G. W. Kinsolving act as Moderator.

"The first meeting of the Presbytery was held at Mt. Zion, according to the above order. All the ordained ministers were present. The licentiates in the bounds of the Presbytery, when first formed, were A. W. Smith, John R. Smith and Thomas Montgomery. W. P. Smith was also received from the Methodist Church as a licentiate, either at the first or second session—the records do not show which. The candidates were M. Dillow, W. P. Baker and N. M. Baker; and Bro. W. C. Russell was received as a candidate at the first session on a letter of recommendation from Pennsylvania Presbytery. Since the organization of the Presbytery it has never failed to meet on its own adjournment twice a year. It has had one called session and two adjourned sessions. It has received as candidates for the ministry twelve persons—ten by experience, viz: J. B. Dickey, T. L. Davis, James Galford, M. K. Demotte, John Elder, J. N. Shelton, John Berg, A. K. Bone, James A. Bone, J. M. Moore; and two by letter, namely, J. B. Hunter and William Sprouse. Of these J. B. Hunter, William Sprouse, T. L. Davis and John Berg were discontinued, and James Galford dismissed by letter.

"There have been nine persons licensed to preach, namely, M. Dillow, W. P. Baker, N. M. Baker, W. C. Russell, J. B. Dickey, M. K. Demotte, J. W. Elder, J. N. Shelton and A. K. Bone. Of these, W. C. Russell was dismissed by letter, and J. B. Dickey died while a licentiate. A. W. Smith, who was a licentiate at the organization, also died without being advanced farther.

"There have been nine persons ordained by the Presbytery, namely, W. P. Smith, John R. Smith, Thomas Montgomery, W. P. Baker, N. M. Baker. M. Dillow, T. G. Stansberry, M. K. Demotte and John Elder. T. G. Stansberry was a licentiate when he united with the Presbytery by letter.

"There were five ordained ministers in the Presbytery at its organization. Nine have been added by ordination, as we have just seen, and fifteen by letter and one by a change in Presbyterial lines, making thirty in all, namely, D. Traughber, J. C. Smith, G. W. Kinsolving, J. B. Lowrance, John Bennett (original members), W. P. Smith, John R. Smith, Thomas Montgomery, W. P. Baker, N. M. Baker, M. Dillow, T. G. Stansberry, M. K. Demotte, John Elder (by ordination), C. Y. Hudson (by a change in lines), and by letter J. D. Cowan, A. J. McGlumphy, William M. Taylor, J. T. A. Henderson, R. G. Carden, R. T. Marlow, J. B. Lowrance, W. L. Bankson, D. R. Bell, James Ashmore, J. M. Bone, H. W. Bryant, Jesse Beals, P. H. Crider and John Crisman. Of this number sixteen have been dismissed by letter, viz.: J. B. Lowrance (twice), G. W. Kinsolving, John Bennett, J. T. A. Henderson, Wm. M. Taylor, R. T. Marlow, Thomas Montgomery, W. P. Baker, A. J. McGlumphy, D. R. Bell, James Ashmore, T. G. Stansberry, R. G. Carden, D. Traughber, J. M. Bone, and H. W. Bryant. Rev. Jesse Beals was transferred to the Hill Presbytery at its organization. Revs. J. R. Smith, J. D. Cowan, W. P. Smith and J. C. Smith have died, and M. K. Demotte has been deposed for immoral conduct. The whole number appears to be thirty, but as Rev. J. B. Lowrance appears both as an original member and as received by letter, it makes the actual total membership twenty-nine. The present roll of the Presbytery is: Ordained ministers, M. Dillow, C. Y. Hudson, W. L. Bankson, P. H. Crider, John Elder, John Crisman, and N. M. Baker; licentiates, J. N.

Shelton, A. K. Bone; candidates, J. M. Moore and James A. Bone.

"There are eleven organized churches now under the care of the Presbytery, viz.: Mt. Zion, Bethany, New Hope, Prairie Hall, Shady Grove, Bethlehem, Madison, Blue Mound, North Fork, Friends Creek, and Dry Ridge. All these congregations have church houses, except Blue Mound and Dry Ridge. The Mt. Zion congregation was organized by Rev. David Foster on the 24th of April, 1830; and the first Sabbath-school in Macon county was organized here in 1831. The church now has about 175 members, and a Sabbath-school of about 70. Bethlehem congregation was organized in 1850 by Rev. J. C. Smith, from members belonging formerly to Mt. Zion and Mt. Carmel congregations. At present it numbers about 100 members, with 60 in Sabbath-school. North Fork was organized by Rev. J. C. Smith in April, 1855, with fifty-four members, all but six of whom had formerly been members at Mt. Zion. Present membership, 52, with 66 in Sabbath-school. Pleasant Grove was organized Oct. 16, 1870, by Rev. W. L. Bankson. Present membership, 78; Sabbath-school, 40. New Hope was organized July 2, 1871, by Rev. C. Y. Hudson. Present membership, 117; Sabbath-school, 40."

### EWING PRESBYTERY.

The following, from Rev. J. L. Riley, explains itself. We are sorry not to have secured a more detailed history of this large and flourishing Presbytery.

"Ewing Presbytery of the Cumberland Presbyterian Church was formed by the action of the Illinois Synod in the Fall of 1844. Rev. Jesse Pearce was appointed Moderator. Its first meeting was held at Village, White county, Ill., in March, 1845. Its ministers were: Revs. Jesse Pearce, John Porter, Richard Harris, John Crawford, Benjamin Bruce, and Moses J. Pearce. Its congregations (several, at least,) were among the first organized in the State. Its probationers were: J. M. Miller, Thos. Joyner, John Brinkley, R. M. Davis, J. A. Porter, Orison Melvin, A. R. Barlow, etc. E. B. Pearce and the writer joined at this meeting. Revs. Jesse Pearce and John Crawford, in particular, were among the laborious itinerants in the early settlement of the country in Southern Illinois. The other four were a little more secularized, but, nevertheless, did much faithful work. Five of them have finished their work and gone to their reward. Rev. John Crawford still lives, and is able to do some preaching and pastoral work. The Barnetts, McLin, and their co-laborers, were instrumental, under God, in introducing Cumberlandism in Southern Illinois. Nearly all the early preachers in this part of the State were probationers under the care of the Anderson Presbytery, in Kentucky, before the organization of the Illinois Presbytery. Rev. David McLin organized the first congregations in this part of the State in 1819. I think their order was as follows: Hopewell, White county; Village, White county; New Pleasant, Gallatin county; and Union Ridge, White county. Village held its first camp-meeting in the fall of 1819, and its last one in 1869, making fifty camp-meetings on that consecrated ground. It is estimated that fifteen hundred souls have embraced religion there; and that not less than twenty-five to thirty of these have gone out from that place to preach the unsearchable riches of Christ.

"There are, within the bounds of this Presbytery, some thirteen ordained ministers, six or eight probationers, something over thirty congregations, and probably a membership of fifteen or eighteen hundred. The sentiments and sympathies of the public, within the operations of our people in this Presbytery, are strongly with us; and if there was more of the spirit of consecration and co-operation upon the part of both preachers and people, our cause might soon become very strong."

## M'LIN PRESBYTERY.

This body was organized at the same time that Ewing Presbytery was, by dividing the old Illinois Presbytery into three. The action of Synod was had in 1844. Accordingly, this Presbytery met on the first Thursday in April, 1845, at Monmouth meeting-house. Rev. Felix G. Trousdale was to be Moderator, and, in case of his absence, Rev. A. L. Hamilton. The Presbytery seems to have been composed of the following ministers: A. L. Hamilton, B. A. Smith, F. G. Trousdale, Woods M. Hamilton, and Wm. Finley. Of these we do not know of one now living. Certainly there are none of them living in the bounds of this Presbytery. All are gone. This Presbytery has churches in the following, among other towns: Salem, Flora, Fairfield, Iuka, Albion, and Kinmundy. It occupies important ground and has a good membership. In our statistical report will be found further definite information concerning this body.

## RUSHVILLE PRESBYTERY.

The following brief sketch has been kindly furnished us by Rev. J. D. Foster, the worthy Stated Clerk. It is very brief, but yet contains items of great interest about some of the early ministers of this Presbytery which we have been able to acquire nowhere else. While we could wish the sketch was more nearly complete, yet we are compelled to give it as the best we have been able to secure.

"Rushville Presbytery was organized March 10, 1836, in the town of Rushville, Schuyler county, Ill., by Revs. John M. Berry, Benjamin Canby, James M. Stockton, and Cyrus Haynes; and elders John M. Barton, William Travers, and Micaiah Warren. The principal actors were John M. Berry, Cyrus Haynes, Abner McDowell, Peter Downey, John Crawford, and Wm. C. McKamy. I know almost nothing of them, having been a member of Presbytery but a few years.

"Cherry Grove Seminary was commenced as a high

school at a very early date, I think. As early, perhaps, as 1840. Presbytery seems to have labored continuously to make it a success up to the time it was given up as a school, in 1866, to make a concentrated effort on Lincoln University.

"As to missions, there have been, it would seem, but two—Peoria and Macomb—both of which are defunct. Having started on the down-grade during the war, they struggled on a few years and then died out.

"As to the old men, Cyrus Haynes, who lived for a number of years in this place (Abingdon), and afterwards at Cherry Grove, preached all over the Presbytery until the year 1849, when he took his letter and, I am informed, located in Iowa. About the time of the war he was in Missouri awhile, and finally died out there about the year 1867 or 1868. Whatever else may be said of him, no one can look over the minutes of the Presbytery during the thirteen years in which he was connected with it, and not feel that he was an earnest, efficient minister. In his 'report' in 1848, he says that he has traveled on foot to reach his appointments about 200 miles. Besides being a preacher, he was an able and successful teacher in the Seminary for a number of years.

"John M. Berry, I doubt not, is known to you as a great preacher, but he does not appear to have continued with the Presbytery long.

"Abner McDowell seems to have been one of their best preachers and most pious men. He died in 1845. He seems to have lived at Rushville from about the time of the organization till his death. In relation to his death the Presbytery resolved, that they had been bereaved of one of their most worthy, active, and much beloved members, one of their wisest counsellors, and one who had endeared himself to them 'by his uniform, upright and consistent conduct, as well as by his burning zeal, his heavenly mindedness, and deep-toned piety. All of these he exhibited not only by his fervent prayers, his pointed and glowing exhortations, his instructive, powerful, and eloquent sermons, but also in his daily walk and common deportment.' This is the view that is almost universal among the older people as to this worthy though somewhat obscure minister.

"Peter Downey was also one of the most able, devoted, and efficient members. He came to the Presbytery about 1837 or 1838, and labored continuously and efficiently until his death in the Spring of 1850. The Presbytery says of him: 'Bro. Downey was a good man, and full of the Holy Ghost, having a burning zeal for his Master's cause, and an untiring energy devoted to the peace and prosperity of the Church of God.' * * Your Committee have learned, with great satisfaction, that Bro. Downey died in the peace of God. He took his departure to the home of the blest at the same house that your reverend body, at its last session, was holding precious communion, in handling the broken body and shed blood of the Son of God.'

"W. S. Campbell, D. D., joined Presbytery about 1844, was licensed in 1845, and ordained in 1846. He has never been connected with any other Presbytery.

"Rev. W. C. McKamy, now the oldest member of Presbytery, has been a member almost ever since its organization."

# CHAPTER VII.

### CENTRAL ILLINOIS SYNOD.

This Synod was composed of two Presbyteries of Illinois Synod and one of Sangamon, and occupies the central part of the State. The General Assembly of 1859, at Evansville, Ind., after a lengthy preamble, setting forth that the two Synods occupied such a large territory that it was inconvenient for the members to attend, adopted the following:

"*Resolved*, That the Presbyteries of Decatur, Vandalia, and Foster, be, and they are hereby constituted a Synod, to be known as Central Illinois Synod; that it hold its first session in the town of Sullivan, Moultrie county, Ill., on Thursday, at 11 o'clock, A. M., before the third Sabbath in October, 1859; and that Rev. J. B. Logan be the first Moderator, and, in case of his absence, Rev. Daniel Traughber."

We regret to say that the records of this and several subsequent sessions of Synod were destroyed in a fire, which consumed the residence of the Stated Clerk some years since. The writer remembers distinctly that the Synod met, according to appointment, in the Cumberland Presbyterian church at Sullivan. The opening sermon was preached by the appointed Moderator, who presided until the Synod was organized by the election of Rev. Daniel Traughber as Moderator. The name of the temporary Clerk is forgotten, but Rev. J. C. Smith was elected Stated Clerk. This

Synod, although the youngest in the State, has never failed to meet and have a quorum for business.

In 1875 the Foster Presbytery was divided, and the Southern portion, with certain congregations and ministers, was henceforth to be called the Hill Presbytery, in honor of Rev. Isaac Hill, one of the first and most useful of our ministers. The St. Louis & Indianapolis railroad is the dividing line between Foster and Hill Presbyteries. The latter Presbytery is weak, but occupies an important country and is making progress. The Church all over this Synod is in a good, healthy state, with some local exceptions. Revs. J. W. Woods, Jesse Beals, Thomas Bailiff, S. W. Goodknight, J. Groves, R. C. Hill, Samuel Landrous, and Barnabas Lyman comprise Hill Presbytery. Licentiate, David Hall. Many of the old members of the Synod have finished their course and gone home, others have moved away, and but few of those remain who bore the burdens and heat of the day in planting our standards in this country. Of those who remain, we mention with a just pride Rev. James Ashmore. Few men in the Church, taking into the account his opportunities, have done more to win souls to Jesus and build up the Church than has this old veteran of the cross. He still enjoys good health, although age and infirmities are gradually creeping upon him. He preaches Christ still with much of his youthful vim and energy, and with good success. Over a large portion of this Synod the names of Ashmore, Knight, and Traughber are household words in the churches. Knight and Traughber have gone home, and Ashmore alone of the three remains in his old territory, to preach the gospel to dying men. Long may he yet be spared to blow the gospel trumpet! A brief sketch of these worthy brethren will be found in another part of this work.

Central Illinois Synod, from her organization. took bold ground in favor of all the enterprises of the Church, and expressed an unequivocal sympathy with all the great moral movements of the country and age. The writer believes that no part of the Cumberland Presbyterian Church, in proportion to numbers and ability, has done, or is now doing, more for missions, education, Sabbath-schools, &c., than the membership of this Synod. They are ever ready to respond to any department of the work of the Church, when convinced that the work proposed is of God and promises success. They are harmonious in their plans and work, and occupy an important portion of the State running across its entire territory, from the Wabash to the Mississippi river.

The following are the statistics of this Synod, as reported at its session in Georgetown, Vermillion county, Oct., 1877: Ministers, 43; licentiates, 5; congregations, 62; elders, 203; deacons, 67; additions for the year, 525; communicants, 3,706; persons in Sabbath-school, 2,734; total contributions for the year, $17,161; value of church property, $127,160. This is evidently under, rather than over, the true figures.

Since its organization in 1859 the Church in this Synod has more than doubled the value of its church property, and largely increased the membership, while it is no exaggeration to say that thousands of the membership have emigrated to other countries. Their places could only be filled by new recruits from the ranks of the enemy, there being but comparatively little emigration of membership from other parts to this portion of Illinois. Churches are found in the cities of Mattoon, Alton, Fairmount, Georgetown, Taylorville, and many other towns and villages, and the membership will compare favorably in point of intelligence and enterprise with any people in the West. In the bounds of the Synod there are fifty-four houses of worship, neat and comfortable, and but few of them embarrassed by debt.

# CHAPTER VIII.

SKETCHES OF SOME OF THE OLDEST CHURCHES IN THE STATE

## MT. PISGAH CONGREGATION, FOSTER PRESBYTERY.

The following is from the pen of Rev. H. J. VanDuyn:

"This congregation was organized by Rev. James Ashmore in the house of Alexander McDonald, three and one-half miles south-west of Georgetown, Ill., March 1st, 1840. The first ruling elders were Richard Swank, Alex. McDonald, and Charles Canaday. The two former have passed from labor to reward; the latter is now a ruling elder in Georgetown congregation

"For a period of about two years this congregation had no regular place of worship. They met in each other's houses and in school houses (though these were extremely scarce) as opportunity afforded. The good Lord often met with them, and many seasons of refreshing from his presence did they enjoy. In the Summer or Fall of 1842 they built themselves a house of worship on what was then known as the old 'camp-ground,' located on the farm of Mr. McDonald near where the church was organized. This was a hewn log structure, and served admirably the purpose for which it was designed. In it they had many precious revivals, and the Lord added to their numbers many, very many such as should be saved. The good results of the efforts here put forth by that devoted band of faithful workers are being felt and seen by the present rising generation, and doubtless will be felt and seen by many who are yet unborn. But time only reveals, as it were, the shadow. Eternity alone can and will sever the veil, and reveal all the good done here. They continued to occupy this house until the Summer of 1854, when they built themselves a new and, for that day, very commodious frame house, two miles west of Georgetown, on one of the most beautiful sites in the State of Illinois. This house was considered a great credit to the congregation and to the community at large. The site was the gift of ruling elders R. Swank and L. Long. The congregation worshiped here, 'beneath their own vine and fig tree,' through various degrees of prosperity and adversity, until the Summer of 1876, when the old house, that had served so good a purpose for twenty-two years, needing repairs, it was decided to tear it down, build a new one on the same site, and call it by the same name. The new house is a beautiful edifice built in modern style, and speaks well for our cause and people in this part of the country.

"The following ministers have furnished them with 'the word' from the date of organization to the present time: Rev. James Ashmore, from organization until March 8, 1869, a period of 29 years; Rev. W. O. Smith, from March 10, 1869, until April 10, 1870; Rev. G. W. Jordan, from April 24, 1870, until Nov. 8, 1870; Rev. W. O. Smith again, from Dec. 4, 1870, until Oct. 22, 1871. By order of Presbytery Rev. James Ashmore took charge again Oct. 24, 1871, and continued one year, making in all 30 years that he had preached to this congregation. Rev. H. H. Ashmore, a son of James Ashmore, now took charge, and continued until April 1, 1876. A part of the time he had associated with him Rev. Thomas Whitlock. Since April 1, 1876, your humble servant has had charge of the congregation, and is now their pastor.

"Names of elders since organization: L. Long, Emanuel Snider, Samuel Hinton, Richard Swank, Jr., J. S. Long, (now a licensed preacher), J. G. Thompson, and John L. Jones (who was licensed to preach, but died during the war). The first three of the above are the present incumbents."

### OLD BEAR CREEK CHURCH.

Rev. E. M. Johnson has kindly furnished the following sketch of this organization:

"In the month of February or March, a few families from the Church in Kentucky and Tennessee agreed to associate themselves together, with a view to the organization of a Cumberland Presbyterian church at some future time. This was in response to a proposition made by Mr. Rice, and took place at the house of Mr. William Robertson, a Presbyterian, who lived about one and one-half miles north of Greenville, Bond county. These are the the names: Robert Paisley, Elizabeth Paisley, Jonathan Berry, Polly Berry, William and Phenly Young. The date of the permanent organization is not given in the old church book, but the name, Bear Creek, was given to the church at the organization or constitution of the first Presbytery in the State, which took place at the house of John Kirkpatrick in Montgomery county, May, 1823.

"The first elders were Robert Paisley, Jonathan Berry and John Kirkpatrick. Mr. Paisley was from a church in Christian county, Ky.; Mr. Berry from Giles county, and Mr. Kirkpatrick from Sugg's creek congregation, Williamson county, Tenn. Joseph McAdams was ordained ruling elder in this congregation in the fall of 1822—the first elder ordained in the congregation. June 21, 1828, R. W. Denny and Michael H. Walker, and May 9, 1830, Thomas Johnson, were ordained. The present board of elders is five in number. In all, this church has had twenty-five ruling elders up to July, 1877.

"This church has had many acting deacons, but it has

never had but five ordained deacons. Four of these are now acting; the other (an old man) is not.

"The church has now about one hundred and fifty members. Green P. Rice had charge of this church four years; Joel Knight for an unknown but a long time; John Barber supplied it frequently and for a long time; A. M. Wilson one year; Joseph Gordon one year; T. K. Hedges one year; J. M. Bone fourteen years; B. H. Blackwell nearly one year; J. W. Blosser nearly six months; D. R. Bell one year, E. R. Rodgers a short time; J. H. Hendrick nearly two years; and the writer has been here nearly one year. Some of the most influential churches in this country are off-shoots of this congregation. We mention Maple Grove, McDavid's Point, Pleasant Prairie, Goshen, and many others. Many churches in the far West have found that their best workers were from the membership of this church."

### BETHANY CONGREGATION.

This interesting sketch was kindly furnished by ruling elder J. F. Knight:

"In the year 1828 Bro. Andrew M. Bone, the father of Rev. J. M. Bone, settled near Shelbyville, Shelby county, Ill. Shelbyville at that time had but one log cabin for a store house. Rev. David Foster, having heard of his having settled here, visited him, and preached in Shelbyville for the people. It is supposed this was the first Cumberland Presbyterian sermon ever preached in all this country. Father Andrew Bone, having only stopped at Shelbyville for a short time, moved to what is now Moultrie county, Ill., in 1829. Rev. David Foster then lived near Decatur, Ill., and father Bone sent for him to come to his neighborhood and preach for the people. There were no mails in this part of the country then; hence, when friend wanted to see friend, or ask for favors, they had to go in person, or send, to make known their wishes. Out of father Bone's and Rev. Foster's labors grew what is now known as Bethany congregation of the Cumberland Presbyterian Church in Moultrie county, Ill. There is but one of the original members of this congregation now living, sister Emaline Ashmore, who is waiting patiently to pass over to the promised inheritance.

"This church was organized out of three families, Bone, Kennedy, and Lansden, in the fall of 1832. These families concluded to have a camp-meeting. It was a new thing, and those who were members of the church and those who were not were interested in the matter, and all turned out to make preparation for the meeting. Some one wanted to know who would keep a boarding camp. One good old brother told the man that everybody who came to meeting would be taken care of without pay. The camp-meeting came on, with only one minister, and that was Bro. Foster. The Lord blessed his and the few brethren's labor, and nearly every body in the country professed religion. After this a church grew into being, as stated above. After the church was organized, father Bone said he had been praying for the Lord to send a few good people into the country, that he and his family might have the benefit of church privileges; but the Lord knew better how to make a church than he did, for he had now taken the material already at hand, and made a church for him.

"In the Fall of 1830 Thomas D. Lansden, an elder of the Cumberland Presbyterian Church, came from Tennessee, and settled in the bounds of this congregation; and he, in connection with other lovers of the Lord Jesus, was determined that the cause of the Redeemer should go forward. Lansden, Bone and Kennedy were the first elders of Bethany congregation. Camp-meetings were held annually every Fall until the Fall of 1860, as nearly as is remembered. On one occasion, in an early day when the brethren were clearing the ground for a camp-meeting, a dear sinner, about seventy years old, was seen with his implements preparing a place for a camp also. One brother says to another, 'Do you see that old sinner preparing to camp, too? The Lord will pay him.' So he did; for he sought the Lord and found him precious to his soul that very meeting.

"It was not uncommon for persons to separate in small companies in the morning and evening, and go to the woods for prayer; and not unfrequently songs and praises to God could be heard in every direction around the camp-ground. Some rejoiced on account of having just been born again, and others over the great deliverance. Thus it is that they that sow to the Spirit shall of the Spirit reap life everlasting. At one of those early camp-meetings every sinner on the ground professed religion, except one, and he left the ground. It is true, however, that the people were not so numerous as at present, but there were enough to hold a camp-meeting.

"In the year 1838 the brethren said they must have a church house. So they met and decided what kind of a house they would have, and, when they had decided, they started to the woods with axes, broad-axes, and prongs, to get out logs and boards for the erection of a church. The church was built with a door in the east, and a plain pulpit in the west end, and a small window at the back of the pulpit. The people had no stoves in those days, but the church must have fire in Winter; so the brethren made what old fogies call hearths. There were two, about four feet square, on which they placed charcoal and put fire to it. A fire made of this material does not create much smoke, but what was created went where it pleased. This house, with some improvement, remained for a church until 1856, when the church now standing was built. Father Robert Crowder, who is a member of our church, and, at that time, was an elder, took the contract for building it at a cost of $2,100, and waited kindly on the church until paid, he and his sons giving liberally for its completion. By the grace of God we are a self-made people, never having had a collection made for us from abroad. God, having been so good and so kind to us, has enabled us to give thousands of dollars to build up Christ's kingdom in other localities.

"The preachers who officiated in building up the cause of Christ in this country were as follows: The two Barbers (father John Barber and his son John), the two Bones, the two Knights. Daniel Traughber, Mr. Wilson, and others, the most of whom have gone to their reward in heaven. In the year 1832 young Barber came and organized a Sunday-school, and there has been one in operation ever since. The number of ministers gone out from this congregation is four: Revs. J. M. Bone, Thomas Bone (dead), Wm. Bankson, and James Freeland. Bro. Freeland was a graduate of Lebanon University, Tenn."

### MT. ZION.

Rev. P. H. Crider furnishes this sketch of Mt. Zion congregation:

"Mt. Zion congregation, Macon county, Ill., was first organized by Rev. David Foster at his own private dwelling about three miles from Mt. Zion. The organization took place on the 24th day of April, 1830, and soon was taken under the care of Sangamon Presbytery. The following are the names of the charter members: Andrew Wilson, Mary Ann Wilson, Alexander Wilson, Nancy Wilson, Catherine Wilson, Allen Travis, Margaret Travis, Alexander W. Bell, Nancy Jane Bell, James D. Campbell, Lavina Campbell, Andrew Davidson, Assenath R. Davidson, John Davidson, Rhoda Davidson, Samuel Davidson, Elizabeth Davidson, Nancy Davidson, Ellen Davidson Black, John Smith, Margaret Smith, Rebecca Travis, David Davis, Polly M. Davis, Wm. D. Baker, Marilla Baker, Robert Smith, Nancy Smith (Traughber), David Foster, Anna Foster, Robert Foster, Margaret Foster, Wm. C. Foster, Isabella Foster, Nancy Allen Foster. Thirty-six names were taken at the organization, April 24, 1830. On the 15th day of June, 1830, the enrolled members met at the house of Rev. David Foster, and selected the following brethren as ruling elders of the congregation: Andrew Wilson, Allen Travis, Robert Smith and Samuel Davidson. On the 30th of April, 1831, Mr. James Scott was chosen ruling elder. In October, 1832, Mr. James Law became a ruling elder. At about the same time John Smith became a ruling elder of this congregation. In June, 1833, Mr. William M. Young was chosen ruling elder.

"After the death of Rev. David Foster, in May, 1833, the congregation was without a pastor or supply for more than a year. During this time the congregation declined in spirituality, which resulted in neglecting the Sabbath-school and the means of grace. After this the labors of Rev. Neill Johnson were secured, who preached for the congregation for one year and six months. The congregation was then without regular preaching until the last of November, 1836, when Rev. Daniel Traughber, of Kentucky Presbytery, settled in the community and supplied the congregation with preaching at the request of the session. In June, 1837, he joined Vandalia Presbytery, and was appointed to supply Mt. Zion congregation, which had, at that time, one hundred and eight members. The session met March 27th, 1856, for the purpose of properly arranging their congregational records, as two new congregations had been stricken off from the membership of Mt. Zion congregation, Bethlehem and North Fork. In fact, about all the congregations in the bounds of Decatur Presbytery have had their origin from the old Mt. Zion congregation. This is one of the places where camp-meetings were kept up for many years. and the results can never be fully known until the revelation of all things at the last day. Thousands will rise up in that day and testify that they were born again at the consecrated altar of old Mt. Zion. This has been a prolific fountain, from whence a stream of Christian influence has gone out in every direction. Her sons and daughters are not confined to the limits of this Presbytery, but many of them have gone to Missouri, Kansas, and other States, and are at work in the Master's cause. But the greater number of those who have been begotten in the gospel at this place have finished their work on earth, and have gone to our Father's house in heaven. Such brethren as the Smiths, Davidson, Wilson, and many others, toiled long and hard at Mt. Zion, and at last died at their post. Many other good brethren and sisters are lingering on the same ground, and, having been 'faithful over a few things,' are watching and waiting for the heavenly welcome.

"The following are the names of the ministers of the gospel who have been pastors and supplies of this congregation since its organization: David Foster (died 1833), Neill Johnson, Daniel Traughber (dead), Samuel Aston (died here Nov. 1856), John T. A. Henderson, R. T. Marlow, T. R. Lester, R. G. Carden (died here July, 1874), N. M. Baker, P. H. Crider. The above have all been pastors and supplies, besides the following, who supplied the pulpit for a few months each at intervening times: J. C. Smith, Abner Lansden, Joseph B. Lowrance, J. D. Cowan, and M. Dillow. During the centennial year of 1876 the congregation repaired their church property to an amount considerably over four hundred dollars. They support the pastor for all his time, and regularly attend to the monthly contribution for missions. Although the congregation has suffered much by removals and deaths, there is a manifest willingness and desire to work for the promotion of the Redeemer's kingdom. The church has, at present, about one hundred and seventy-five members, and a Sabbath-school of about seventy-five pupils, with eight teachers. The first Sabbath-school in this (Macon) county was organized at this place by Rev. David Foster in 1831. The first superintendent was James Scott, and the assistant was Andrew Wilson. The first sermon in this county by a Cumberland Presbyterian was preached by Rev. John M. Berry in an old log school house three and a half miles southwest of Decatur."

# CHAPTER IX.

LETTERS FROM VARIOUS BRETHREN IN REFERENCE TO THE EARLY TIMES OF THE CHURCH IN ILLINOIS.

We think it best, at the risk of some repetition in relation to some things in the first years of the Church, to let the following brethren speak for themselves, in their own language and in their own style. We feel sure these letters will repay a careful reading and re-reading. The writers were eye-witnesses of much of which they write, and, being now far advanced in life, they were themselves actors, in large part, in the scenes so vividly described. First, we introduce to the reader the very interesting letter of Rev. Neill Johnson, of McMinnville, Oregon, to whom we are largely indebted for many facts already referred to in the fore part of this volume, and who, in a ripe old age, still lives to work for the Master with marked vigor. What is here recorded from his pen was sent at different times, but we shall publish his letters as one continued narrative.

"God, in his providence, overruled that roving, restless disposition, said to be peculiar to the American people, for building up his cause and lengthening the cords of his Church; and the first stakes in nearly every place where we subsequently formed an organization were set by one or more ruling elders or prominent church members. These sent pressing and earnest calls back to their former pastors or ministers for the preaching of the word and the ordinances of the Church. These calls never failed to touch a tender cord in the heart of the called minister, who, in that day, did not wait to learn how much could be raised to sustain him, or whether anything could be even promised. Had they done this, many places that now have well paid pastors and church houses would still be a barren waste, at least so far as Cumberland Presbyterians are concerned. Of these prominent members and ruling elders I will name John Hamilton and Judge Taylor, who settled first near Golconda, in the extreme southern part of the State, and, after an organization had been effected there, they both removed—the former to Morgan county and the latter to Sangamon. Mr. Hamilton was a well informed theologian, and very able in prayer and exhortation. I doubt not many stars will be in his crown in that great day. On the Mauvaisterre, where he settled, a flourishing congregation was built. We had several very interesting camp-meetings there, but owing to removals, and other causes, I think to-day we have no organization near there. Mr. Hamilton died in a good old age, and was gathered to his people. Bro. Taylor aided in building up a church on Spring Creek. Subsequently he removed to Rushville, where he again witnessed a revival and saw a flourishing congregation built up. There he remained till his Master called him.

"At Golconda, or near there, where we first noticed these brethren, we have still an organization. Bro. Thomas Campbell first settled there when a licentiate, and removed with Judge Taylor. They settled near each other on Spring Creek, where Bro. Campbell remained till his death, which took place very suddenly over twenty-five years ago. Here I will relate an incident which I learned from Francis Dodds, of Kentucky. At an early day, when the cry for ministers and ministerial labors were very pressing, the Synod appointed a day of fasting and prayer for the special purpose of asking God to send more laborers into his vineyard. The congregation met at Bethlehem meeting house, and a solemn time it was, said my informant. Many fervent prayers were offered that God would send men of his own choosing to proclaim salvation to a dying world. Says he, 'I had in my mind young men, educated men, and men at a distance; but there was my neighbor, Thomas Campbell, a very devoted, pious man, somewhat advanced in life, with a large family. I never once thought of his being called; but when Presbytery met, some half dozen or more came forward, Bro. Campbell among the rest, and there was not a man among them that proved to be more humble, holy, or useful than he became.'

### STOUTS GROVE.

"The first attempt at an organization in all the region now embraced in Mackinaw and Decatur Presbyteries, was in the Fall of 1829. At the time of which I write there were a few families of our church settled in Stouts Grove, then Tazewell county, now McLean county. These were the McClure connections and Peyton Mitchell. They desired a camp-meeting, which was held by Rev. J. M. Berry, Thomas Campbell and Gilbert Dodds. My brother, Archibald Johnson, and I were also present—I a licentiate and my brother a candidate. The meeting was an interesting one. At its close there was a universal petition for an immediate organization. Accordingly, Bro. Berry led in the matter, and members were received who were scattered over a territory more than fifty miles in diameter, and elders chosen and ordained, such as had not been previously ordained. They lived so remote from each other that it was not expected they would all get together more than once a year. They were expected and charged individually to watch over the members in their several regions. All of these elders, with one exception, have gone to their eternal reward. No two of them lived nearer each other than ten or fifteen miles. All of them, however, lived in important neighborhoods, and were calling urgently for preaching. At that time, however, there was not an ordained preacher living in the entire bounds of what we then called Stouts Grove congregation. There was one licentiate (myself), and two candidates, Peyton Mitchell and my brother, Archibald Johnson. Bro. Mitchell was, at the time of which we are writing, about forty years of age. He was of a very intelligent, high-minded family, a son of Col. Mitchell, of the revolution, and a brother of the late professor, Gen. Mitchell, of the Union army. All his family connections were of Presbyterian parentage, and he was a member of McGready's congregation in Kentucky. He himself, however, I think, was the only one of his father's family that ever united with the Cumberland Presbyterians."

### PEYTON MITCHELL.

"Here I will relate an incident which I got from father Roleofson: It is a matter of history that Mr. McGready, on his death-bed or near the time of his death, advised his people to unite with the Cumberland Presbyterians; and, accordingly, they held a camp-meeting in the Roleofson settlement, near where Mr. Mitchell lived. He had never had any acquaintance with our Church at this time, and his prejudices were all against us. Being well acquainted with father Roleofson, and knowing him to be warm, and as he considered, enthusiastic, he took him to one side before there had been any preaching, and warned him that they should be careful and not readily fall in with a people that were considered disorderly. The first man that occupied the stand was Rev. Robert Morrow. As he said afterwards, he looked upon him as contemptible, young, beardless, stoop-shouldered, and hump-backed; but when Mr. Morrow began, his voice was clear and melodious, his arguments logical and exactly to the point. Mr. Mitchell drew nearer and nearer, till, at the close of the sermon, he was standing near and facing Mr. Morrow with mouth open and eyes streaming with tears. The whole congregation, saints and sinners, were moved in a manner which cannot be described intelligibly to one who has not witnessed something similar. From that time Mr. Mitchell was a Cumberland Presbyterian. He became a candidate for the ministry at the first meeting of the Illinois Presbytery. Few, if any, of the ministry believed that he had preaching talents, and yet he exerted an influence in that direction that did much in opening the way for others to do good. He was of an agreeable, social turn of mind, and possessed conversational powers seldom surpassed by our best preachers. He was finally licensed, but never ordained. He was the first one to introduce Cumberland Presbyterians in what was afterwards Sandy Creek congregation, and perhaps in some other places."

### ARCHIBALD JOHNSON.*

"I now pass to give a brief sketch of the life and labors of my own dear brother, Archibald Johnson. He was the youngest of eight children. His grandfather emigrated from Tyrone county, Ireland, early in the eighteenth century, and settled in the bounds of Barbacas congregation, Cumberland county, N. C. Our mother was a native of Jura, Scotland, and came to America about the same time. Her maiden name was McDuffer. Our parents were married in the aforesaid congregation, and there all the children of our family were born, but the subject of this notice. He was born in Christian county, Ky., on the 26th of April, 1807. In his childhood he had severe fits, but they left him at about three years of age. Till about seven years of age he was remarkably careless. He had neither taste nor inclination for books, and, although he never was given to falsehood or profanity, he had no inclination to religion. At about the

---

*We could not extract these sketches and place them with other sketches without marring, somewhat, the symmetry of the letter. Hence, they are found here.

age of seven years he suddenly became as remarkable for his love of books and study as he had before been careless and inattentive; and this followed him to the last of life.

"The first lasting religious impression made upon him was at a public examination (common in that day), at which the adult members of the church were examined on theological questions predicated on some one or more questions in the Catechism, and the children of the church were examined on the Catechism at large. My brother readily answered all the questions asked him on the Catechism. At the close the minister, Rev. Wm. Barnett, propounded a personal question to each child, and then there followed a powerful exhortation. The question put to my brother was: 'Do you ever pray?' He dropped his head. He said afterwards: 'I felt that I dared not tell a lie.' He answered, 'No, sir.' Then followed an exhortation of a powerful character, fastening conviction, from which he never got clear till it terminated in a sound conversion. His conversion took place at a camp-meeting in Illinois in 1822. While many were down crying for mercy, a friend in whom he had confidence went to him and asked him to bow in prayer. This he did, and there made a vow that he would never leave that spot until he got an evidence of pardon, or became satisfied there was no pardon for him. In after life he seriously condemned this course as rash and unauthorized. He remained there, however, till the congregation dispersed, and he was removed, unwillingly, into a camp. There the tempter suggested to him he had now broken his vow, and, like Annanias and Sapphira, he had lied to God, and now there was no mercy for him. Here he sank into the most gloomy depair. He told a friend there was no use in praying for him or in his praying: that his damnation was forever sealed. His friend told him, no; that the very fact of his being alive and out of hell was evidence that God had not yet cut him off from his mercy; and quoted to him that not a sparrow can fall without his notice or permission. At this he seemed to catch. His mind was directed in this wise: if God catches the falling, worthless sparrow, will he not catch and save the falling sinner for whom Christ died, who casts himself wholly upon him? Yes, he will. 'Here,' said he, 'I was enabled to put my trust wholly on him who watches over even a worthless, helpless sparrow, and more particularly a worthless, helpless, falling sinner.' He was now fifteen years old. He seemed to be impressed to warn sinners of their danger, and began without delay to urge those of his own age and younger to come to Christ.

"He joined Illinois Presbytery in the Fall of 1827. He made rapid progress in study until April, 1830, when he and his friends expected he would be licensed and placed on a circuit. But, contrary to this expectation, the Presbytery, on a close vote, did not sustain his piece, and ordered him to write again from the same text. He returned home very gloomy and cast down, thinking the Presbytery had no confidence in him. In this, however, he was mistaken. For a while he gave up the idea of preaching, went to farming, and made an engagement to get married. He did not attend Presbytery in the Fall, but in the Spring of 1831, at the earnest solicitation of a friend who had always exercised a great influence over him, he attended, and was licensed.

"In the Fall of 1830,

### JAMES E. DAVIS,

a licentiate, moved from Southern Illinois, and settled near what is now Hopedale. He professed religion early in life, and had deep impressions that it was his duty to preach, but never joined Presbytery till the Fall of 1823, the second meeting of Illinois Presbytery. He was then some forty years of age, had but little education, had a large family, and pecuniarily was only in moderate circumstances. He was licensed in 1825, and was ordained by the Sangamon Presbytery in 1834. He was able in prayer and exhortation, and had a few discourses that he preached acceptably and ably. He went several times to the General Assembly. He lived to a good old age, raised a respectable family, several of whom died before he did."

### A BRIEF SKETCH OF THE ELDERSHIP OF STOUTS GROVE CONGREGATION.

"The first congregation, as I have said, in the bounds of what subsequently became Mackinaw Presbytery, was organized by Rev. J. M. Berry in the Fall of 1829, at the close of a camp-meeting in Stouts Grove. All the first elders, with the exception of Joel Hargrove, have been removed by death, some of them many years ago. Bro. Hargrove, however, has resided on the Pacific Coast over twenty years. He is now eighty-two years old. I saw him at the meeting of Oregon Synod in November last, as a member from Cascades Presbytery. He is hale and hearty, and, to all appearances, bids fair for twenty or more years. He has resided in several localities, both on this coast and in the Atlantic States, and has been active, pecuniarily, in organization and in maintaining doctrine and discipline in a half dozen or more congregations. Few, if any, have done more pecuniarily to sustain an evangelical ministry than Bro. Hargrove. While in the Atlantic States he was a representative in the General Assembly several times.

"Thomas McClure and Robert Bird were considerably advanced in life at the time of which I now write. Both were converted in the celebrated revival of 1800. Neither of them possessed advantages of more than a common education, such as could be obtained in the back woods of Kentucky at any early day. They were men, however, of good common sense and of undoubted piety, and had the entire confidence of the community where they lived. One instance of Bro. Bird's ready wit: A Universalist minister was boasting to him of the progress his church was making, and their increase in numbers. 'I believe,' said Mr. Bird, 'the devil himself was a Universalist preacher, and the first sermon that we have an account of him preaching was in the Garden of Eden. His text was: 'For God doth know that in the day thou eatest thereof thou shalt not surely die.' He began by denying what God had said, and all the ministers of your church follow in his footsteps.' Father Bird and his aged companion both died in Oregon several years ago. Father McClure died on his old homestead near where our first organization in this region was made. His aged companion, a true mother in Israel, survived him several years. I believe all their children were pious. A few were living, at the last account, but most of them were gone. The church in and around Stouts Grove still lives, and I believe prospers; and when God writes up his people it shall be said, as of Zion of old, 'This and that man was born there.'

"James McClure, much like his father, lived a pious life and died a happy death. His widow survived him, but he left no children.

"Archie Bryan was an elder brother of Dr. Alfred Bryan. He was a very useful, pious man, and lived to see a congregation organized near him. Lincoln University is in the vicinity where he lived and died. 'He, being dead, yet speaketh.'

"Ebenezer Craig lived long enough to see two or three congregations not far distant from where he lived and died; but his labors ended many years since.

"Mr. Guthrie is now the only elder above named whose history remains to be noticed. He lived in a sparsely settled region at that time, and I am not sure that he was ever visited by any of our ministers. He stood nominally attached to our Church for several years, attending, with his family, our annual camp-meeting in Stouts Grove. They, however, finally joined the Methodist Church, and one or two of his sons became prominent ministers in that denomination.

"With the exception of the last elder named, all of those embraced in the organization of Stouts Grove lived to see organizations in their immediate vicinities. Some of them remain to the present day. One only (Sand Prairie), where we had several camp-meetings and saw some lasting good done, has since ceased to be. Deaths, removals, and other causes, combined to remove the candlestick. But still, in other places besides these, God blessed the self-denying efforts of a few toiling, mostly unremunerated, self-denying ministers in planting our standard in what was then a new country. A few in Oregon, the writer among the number, are duplicating what we experienced in that early day. Reader, compare the condition of the Cumberland Presbyterian Church at the time of which I am now writing with the present, and then exclaim: 'What hath God wrought!' But we still have faith that God will bless the poor labors of his poor servants in Oregon as he has done in Illinois; and to all eternity he shall have the glory."

#### LETTER FROM REV. J. W. WOODS.

"I think it was in the year 1821 that Richard Armstrong, who was a convert during the great revival under McGready's preaching, moved into Clark county, this State, and became a nucleus around which gathered one of the most useful congregations of this State. In 1825 there were eleven church members in the family, embracing two sons-in-law. At that time my father moved in, and the next year there was an organization, Rev. John M. Berry officiating. Several ministers had visited them before this—Maryweather, one or two of the Downeys, and perhaps Hunter and others.

"There should be more than a passing notice of Richard Armstrong, for he withstood an unusually strong tide of persecution from the old church. No occurrence of the kind, as given in Alice McDonald, surpasses it. There was a strong organization there, embracing nearly all the intelligence of the country, when he came in. I recollect him making this remark at one time to my father: 'I shall have no more trouble from these people. The Lord has bridled them. They must stop. The Lord will give me triupmh over them.' I was then a little boy, but a decided impression was made on my mind, and I looked on and remembered as the years rolled away. It was realized to the letter. Some died; some removed to Coles county and there acknowledged our doctrines; and some who remained became convinced they were of God, and a few came into the Church. Nearly all of their children became converts in the end. Richard Armstrong lived to see a strong church built up, and five or six more organized, in whole or in part the outgrowth of old Big Creek church. As an elder he traveled into Vermillion, Coles, Macon, Fayette, Shelby, Bond, and other counties."

### LETTER FROM REV. R. D. TAYLOR.

"Revs. Neill and Archibald Johnson, James E. Davis, James McDowell, and Peyton Mitchell (licentiate) were here when I came to the State of Illinois in 1836. They were all faithful servants of the Church, laboring day and night for the salvation of sinners, and God greatly blessed their labors. Well do I remember with what zeal and power they preached the gospel. In those early days there were but few church houses. We had generally to depend upon log school houses, barns, and the shady groves. Campmeetings were the order of the day from the month of August to the last of October. Scores were converted at these meetings. Hundreds came from a distance of forty and fifty miles. They generally commenced on Friday and closed on the following Tuesday morning. Out of the labors of these faithful men of God congregations were organized over many portions of what is now known as Mackinaw Presbytery. Most of the old ministers and elders of those days have gone to their reward in heaven. Truly it may be said of them, 'Blessed are the dead which die in the Lord from henceforth; yea, saith the Spirit, that they may rest from their labors, and their works do follow them.'

"My father and mother were both members of the Beech congregation of the Cumberland Presbyterian Church, Sumner county, Tenn. They were converts of the revival of 1800. My father, Robert Taylor, was a ruling elder of the above-named congregation, in which capacity he served until the day of his death. My mother's maiden name was Margaret Kirkpatrick, sister of the Rev. Hugh Kirkpatrick. My father was born in Pennsylvania; my mother in South Carolina. They died full of years, in hope of a blessed immortality and eternal life beyond the grave. They were buried in the Beech cemetery, near the old Beech stone church, of precious memory. I have often heard my father speak of the organization of our church: how he had entertained all the first ministers around his table at the same time. He had a good opportunity to be conversant with their trials and discouragements. But never did I hear him intimate that our fathers in the ministry ever made any proposition to unite with the Methodist Episcopal Church, as related by Dr. Cartwright. If there had ever been such a proposition my father certainly would have known something about it, and I would most certainly have heard him speak of it. I was born in Sumner county, Tenn., Feb. 17, 1814. I professed religion about the year 1826 under the labors of Revs. Francis Johnson and Eli Guthrie, at a camp-meeting at Mt. Moriah. No instrumentality was more efficient, under God, in my salvation than the prayers of my father. At an early day after my conversion I was strongly impressed with the duty of preaching the gospel, but, being unwilling to enter upon that duty, I chose the profession of medicine.

In view of that profession, when about eighteen years old I entered Cumberland College. There, among strangers and in a strang land, I was more and more impressed with the duty of preaching the gospel. Neither time nor place had made any change in my mind. Such was my state of mind, in a great measure I lost the enjoyment of religion. I often feared that I had never been converted. I could not pursue my studies in College with any satisfaction; and, with a mind dark as midnight, I kept my own impressions of duty to myself. I made no man my counsellor, having settled upon my profession before I entered College. I supposed all were in profound ignorance of my state of mind; and if I did not believe in a special call to the gospel ministry, the whole matter, up to this day, would be to me a profound mystery. Princeton Presbytery having met in College (I cannot definitely mention the date), Dr. Beard came to my room and informed me that he wished to speak to me privately. To my great surprise, he informed me that if I wished to unite with Presbytery I could now have the opportunity. I went with him. After a full relation of my feelings, I was received as a candidate for the ministry under the care of the Princeton Presbytery, and Psalm cxlv. 20 was assigned me as a text to prepare a written discourse upon for next Presbytery. In the Spring of 1836, in the city of Princeton, Ky., I was duly licensed to preach the gospel by Princeton Presbytery, wherever God in his providence might cast my lot. The same Spring I was licensed I came to Illinois, and in 1837 was ordained to the whole work of the ministry by the Presbytery of Mackinaw. My whole life, from the time I united with Presbytery, has been particularly devoted to the interest of the Church. On the 8th of August, 1837, I was united in marriage to Martha A. Robbins by Rev. James E. Davis in the town of Marion, Ill."

# CHAPTER X.

## MISSIONS AND PUBLICATION.

In an important sense, nearly all the work done in the State, until within a few years, was mission work. When the writer first became acquainted with the Church in Illinois (1853)—and his position enabled him to know—there was not a congregation in the State wholly sustaining a pastor. The whole field was missionary ground.

At an early day the Board of Missions, at Lebanon, Tenn., established a mission at Peoria, and not long after sent a missionary to Macomb. Rev. S. T. Stewart was the missionary to the former place for some years. He organized a small congregation, and there was built a house of worship, and for a time there seemed to be a good prospect of success. He finally resigned, and accepted the charge of the church in Pittsburgh, Pa., as pastor. The congregation in Peoria was left for a time without a pastor. Then the war came on and further demoralized the little flock.

In 1863 the General Assembly appointed a missionary committee at Alton, to act in the place of the Board of Missions located at Lebanon, Tenn., from which the missions in Illinois were now separated by the war. This committee existed two years, and then was organized by the Assembly of 1865 into a regular Board consisting of thirteen members.

The missions in Illinois, and all north of Tennessee, were turned over to this Board. Peoria had been without a missionary for more than a year before the committee existed. They found the little flock scattered and greatly discouraged. To get a man for the place seemed next to impossible. The war was raging in all its fury. Finally Rev. L. W. Sayers, of Pennsylvania, was secured. He was a worthy man and a good preacher. Under his labors the mission began to revive, and strong hopes were entertained of its success, when he was prostrated by sickness from which he never recovered. After the death of Mr. Sayers, it seemed impossible to secure a supply. The Board reported to the Assembly in 1865 that the mission had been without a missionary for over two years, and they had despaired of procuring one. In the meantime, deaths and removals had almost annihilated the little band at Peoria. The Sangamon Synod, by whom the enterprise had been started, finally took entire control of the mission, but never succeeded in reviving it. The property was finally sold, and the enterprise abandoned. Had it not been for the war, we do not doubt success would have crowned the enterprise.

Macomb mission went in the same way, except that the house is still preserved. It seemed impossible to get suitable men and means for these points at that day.

Mattoon was also for some time a mission point, receiving counsel and help from the Board. The congregation is still living, with a good house of worship.

Atlanta is another point which was, for a time, nominally under the Board's care. Rev. J. E. Roach was the missionary. He was to receive all the funds contributed by Mackinaw Presbytery. The congregation is still living, with a good house of worship, but at present is unsupplied.

Perhaps the mission which engaged most attention, and had the hardest struggle, was the Alton mission. It was started by Vandalia Presbytery. As early as 1848 they formed a Presbyterial Missionary Society, auxiliary to the Assembly's Board. Shortly after, Rev. A. M. Wilson was employed as traveling missionary at $200 per annum. In the Fall of 1850 this Society paid Mr. Wilson and had $36.41 left in the treasury. The missionary had traveled and preached over a large area, and had succeeded well. In closing up the report of the Treasurer the Secretary records: "He also reports a subscription paper for the special purpose of raising means for sustaining a missionary in Alton; that there is on said paper $51.50 subscribed, $5 of which is paid." This seems to have been the beginning of the Alton mission. At this same meeting Mr. Wilson, the missionary, was instructed to take subscription for the Alton enterprise; and the Secretary, Rev. Joel Knight, was to present the matter to Synod, and try to enlist that body in the enterprise. At every subsequent semi-annual meeting the matter was discussed with increased interest, until the Fall of 1853, when Rev. T. H. Hardwick was employed to go to Alton and begin operations as a missionary. Mr. Wilson was now residing in Upper Alton, and proposed to board any missionary gratis for a year. Mr. Hardwick, having no family, was engaged for $300 per annum, exclusive of board. He entered upon his work Dec. 1, 1853, and continued one year. During this time he, assisted by others, held a meeting of much interest in the town of Upper Alton, at which there were over thirty professions of religion, and twenty-six persons gave their names to form a congregation. But Mr. Hardwick became dissatisfied when the year expired, declined a re-engagement, and went to the State of Texas, where, a few years after, he died.

From the Fall of 1854 to the Spring of 1855 Rev. A. M. Wilson supplied the mission. In the Spring of 1855 the writer removed his family from St. Louis to lower Alton—which is Alton proper—in order to secure a more healthy position for his family, while publishing, in St. Louis, the *Missouri Cumberland Presbyterian*. He was solicited to take charge of the mission, and agreed to do so till some missionary could be obtained, he spending all his Sabbaths and one-half of his week time serving the mission, and to receive for his services $600. The following June he organized a little congregation of eighteen members in the German church on Henry street, with William Blair and Benjamin Rose as elders. Trustees were also elected, a lot bought, and a church house begun, the basement of which was so far completed that the little flock held their first meeting in it the first Sunday in January, 1856. The second Sunday the Sunday-school was organized, with Stephen Lufkin as Superintendent. It had twenty-five to thirty members. The next Spring the audience room was completed, and was dedicated in June. The whole cost—embracing lot, fencing and house—was over $5,200. A debt was left on it of full one-half this sum. When the first year expired (we quote from the records of the Presbyterial Society which employed the missionary), "it was found, on examination, that the missionary had received during the last year $282, which was a little short of one-half the salary he proposed to labor for. He, Rev. J. B. Logan, proposed, in order to disembarrass the Board, to make a sacrifice of one half ($300) for his past services."—Miss. Soc. records, page 35. That is, the writer gave them, the first year of his services, three hundred dollars to sustain that enterprise. It was do this, or place the whole work done in jeopardy. We may say, also, that we paid this first year for the single item of house rent $250, being within $50 of our entire salary. Besides this, we had already given to the church house fund $100, and supplemented it with $150 more during the second and third years. We record these items, not out of any spirit of egotism, but to show what poor missionaries in our Church have passed through. In making our own we are making, in substance, a record for many others. Better days are upon us now—thank God!—but it is well not to forget these times of past hardship and trial.

God blessed the mission with his favor. Souls were converted, and a number added each year. But they were mostly of the poor class; and while the membership increased and the spiritual work went on hopefully and, many times, gloriously, the missionary's salary was *never fully paid*. He sometimes lacked fifty dollars, sometimes a larger amount. The war, in 1861, found us with a good and increasing membership; but, cut off, as we were, from the parent Board, from which we received quarterly fifty dollars, we had only $300 subscribed by our membership, of which all was not realized. Worse still, our church debt was near $2,300, bearing ten per cent. interest. Five hundred dollars of the money was borrowed in a place, and the missionary's name was to all of the notes. It was a dark day. We shall never forget it. But God heard prayer and sent deliverance. Good brethren in the country, without being asked, sent us wagon loads of provisions; and we employed R. M. Beard, of Abingdon, then quite a young man, to enlist as agent to get means to pay the church out of debt. In less than a year, with what he raised in the country and we in the city, we got every dollar and paid every note, and that, too, while the war was upon us in all its fury. During the war God poured out his Spirit, and every year witnessed a glorious revival of religion. Up to the year 1870 there had been *over seven hundred professions of religion in that church, and between four and five hundred had been received on examination*. After the war closed, certain kinds of business which had been flourishing in the city were transferred to St. Louis, and the congregation lost more by removals in a year than were added by examination. In one year over thirty were dismissed by letter, and among them were some of the principal men of means. So the church was destined to another painful trial. Two or three other leading business men died. To complicate the trouble, an improvement was suggested by one or two men, and finally agreed to by the trustees, which necessitated borrowing $2,500 in money. The improvement was made, and the debt has long been an incubus, but, at present writing, seems in a fair way to be extinguished.

In 1871 the writer, after serving the congregation from its organization, resigned. His resignation was refused by a unanimous vote, and a written protest addressed him in very strong and affectionate language. But, after supplying them another year, they yielded to his request, and employed another. They have been served a short time by Revs. J. T. May, J. W. Blosser, and J. H. Hendrick respectively. Though much smaller in number than they were once, yet they have a good Sunday-school and prayer-meeting, and are a live people yet.

### ITINERANT WORK.

Although there is not the missionary work done in the State now in this form that was performed in earlier days, yet several of the Presbyteries do have one or more traveling missionaries in the field, and a good work is done thereby.

### BOARD OF MISSIONS.

As already stated, the General Assembly in 1863 appointed a standing Committee on Missions, which was located at Alton, Ill., composed of the following members: F. Lack, St. Louis, Mo.; D. R. Bell, Otterville, Ill.; J. H. Murphy, Alton, Ill.; R. B. Crossman, Alton; J. B. Logan, Alton; J. M. Bone, Donnellson, Ill.; J. H. Nickell, H. W. Eagan, Salem, Ill.; Isham Finch, Otterville, Ill.; James Bellas, Alton; and G. W. Montgomery, Windsor, Ill. This Committee organized by electing Rev. F. Lack Chairman, and Rev. J. B. Logan Secretary. J. H. Murphy, Esq., was Treasurer. The General Assembly of 1865 turned this Committee into a regular Board of Missions, composed of the following members: J. B. Logan, S. P. Greenwood, Isham Finch, F. Lack, F. Bridgeman, D. R. Bell, P. G. Rea, J. C. Bowdon, W. B. Farr, S. Richards, H. W.

Eagan, and R. S. Reed. They organized by electing J. B. Logan President, H. W. Eagan Secretary, S. P. Greenwood Treasurer. With slight changes in the membership, this Board continued at Alton until the action of the General Assembly in 1869 consolidated the Boards, and located the united Board at St. Louis.

Its existence at Alton was, Committee and Board together, for the term of six years. It did not do a great work, and yet it did something to keep alive missions established in the northern part of the Church, and also did something to beget and cultivate the spirit of missions in the churches. Some of its members were still continued as members of the new Board at St. Louis. If the future reader of history does not find its work very extensive and fruitful, he must remember that it operated in times when it was difficult, if not impossible, to get harmony of sentiment and action from the churches on any subject. Men's minds were unduly excited by the war. Political prejudices caused many to array themselves against the Board, and others were indifferent. In some quarters the Board was put down as "pro slavery," and sympathizing with the rebellion. In other places they were regarded as ultra "radicals," and therefore no help was afforded. But we take great pleasure in here recording that, although there were in the Board men of the most opposite and positive views about the war, these were never introduced into our counsels nor spoken of at our meetings; and the charges from all sides, respecting the Board being controlled in any degree by political sentiment or bias, were certainly unjust and unfounded. The writer was honored as President throughout the entire six years, and knows whereof he affirms. These men met regularly once a month, and counseled and prayed together as brethren, and parted when the Board was dissolved, without a single word having ever been introduced on these subjects, even remotely, in all our six years' intercourse. Warm, earnest discussions there were, animated debates, wide differences of opinion held and expressed, but these discussions and debates and differences were all pertaining to our missionary work—how we could best promote and prosper it. The war, and political issues of any kind, never entered into our conversations or work. As a Board we honestly and faithfully did what we could, and the writer believes that at least the *spirit* of missions was kept up, and, to a degree, cultivated by this Board as not before, at least in our northern territory.

### PUBLICATION.

In the Winter of 1855 and 1856, perhaps in the month of February, 1856, the *Missouri Cumberland Presbyterian*, before published in St. Louis, was removed to Alton, and published there until the following June. This paper was started by the writer in the city of Lexington, Mo., in April of 1852, at the earnest request of leading men all over that State. After publishing in Lexington about one year, we removed to St. Louis in April, 1853, the facilities for such work being every way superior in St. Louis. We resided here two years, during which time constant sickness in the family, resulting in the death of one member, determined us to seek a home for the family out of the city, if possible. Accordingly, on the 15th day of March, 1855, we removed to the city of Alton, after having taken the remains of a dear boy thither to be buried. Seeing the facilities for printing, mailing and transporting a newspaper were just as good in Alton as in St. Louis, and the expense much less, we removed the material and office to Alton in February following. In May, 1857, while at the General Assembly in Huntsville, Ala., we sold our list to A. F. Cox, who was publishing the *Watchman and Evangelist* in Louisville, Ky. The conditions of the trade were, that the two lists were to be united and brought to St. Louis, and that Rev. Dr. Bird was to be editor of the united paper. This was accomplished. Dr.

Bird remained editor, however, only one year. We published the *Missouri Cumberland Presbyterian* six years, and when it was turned over to Mr. Cox we were issuing about three thousand copies. Considering the fact that when we began we were totally inexperienced in newspaper editing and publishing, and the entire territory from which we were to receive our patronage was sparsely settled, the churches poor, weak, scattered and untrained, we have always regarded the success as rather remarkable.

Shortly after selling the weekly, Rev. W. W. Brown, then residing near Alton, and the writer purchased the list of the *Ladies' Pearl* from Rev. W. S. Langdon, at Nashville, and published this ladies' monthly in Alton with encouraging results, until the breaking out of the war in 1861 compelled us to suspend it. It had a good list of subscribers and correspondents, and was gaining ground fast.

From June, 1861, to June, 1862, the war raged in great fury. The writer was struggling with his mission, then having only a handful of members and they poor. But in the Spring of 1862 he was urged by a large number of ministers throughout Illinois, Iowa and elsewhere to publish some sort of a Church paper, as a medium of communication and counsel during those dark and terrible days. We finally consented, although we had not a dollar on earth to start it with, and newspapers by the score had been ceasing all over the country. However, relying on the direction of the "high and holy one," we made the venture, and issued the *Western Cumberland Presbyterian* in the month of June, 1862. It seemed a necessity at the time; but the high prices of paper and all kinds of material used for publishing, added to the fact that the proprietor had to borrow money at a high interest to start and support it for two years, and the additional fact, that he had charge of a mission church not rendering even half a support to his family, made it an exceedingly dangerous experiment. Three denominational papers in St. Louis had suspended. But a kind Providence seemed to smile upon the new undertaking, and it increased in patronage until, had it not been for the large debt incurred in starting it, it would in two years have paid its way, and a handsome profit besides.

In 1866 we sold the list and material to T. H. Perrin, retaining the editorship until 1868, when Rev. J. R. Brown, D. D., bought half the interest in it. The writer then bought the list of the *Cumberland Presbyterian* from A. B. Miller, D. D., and the two lists were united at Alton. Brown, Perrin & Logan were to be the firm. We were to be equal partners, and Mr. Brown and the writer were to be co-editors. This continued but a short time, when the writer sold all his interest in the concern to Brown & Perrin, and retired from the paper. It is but due to truth to say, that we could have sold several times to other parties for a larger price, had we consented to have the paper removed to another part of our Church territory. But believing that we were in duty bound to publish in Alton or St. Louis, as all the subscribers had been obtained with that proposal published to the world, we could not feel that we had any legal or moral right to transfer this list to any other locality.

When the two lists were united the term "Western" as a prefix was dropped by mutual consent, and the united paper called simply the *Cumberland Presbyterian*. Dr. Brown continued to edit the paper after the withdrawal of the writer, and Brown & Perrin to publish it, until it had as large, if not the largest list in the denomination. It was enlarged and improved, was a universal favorite with the Church in the Northwest until its removal to Nashville. It served a noble purpose and did a good work. It was the medium of counsel and encouragement in planning and setting on foot Lincoln University. It is more than questionable in the mind of the writer whether it was possible ever to have successfully planned and started the University, without the advantages of this medium, or another like it. During the dark and exciting years of the war, the writer and some of his correspondents may not always have expressed themselves as discreetly as they ought on the troublous questions which were ever agitating the Church and country. No doubt errors and blunders were made; but he did the best he knew, and hopes—yea, believes—that, notwithstanding mistakes, the benefits received from the paper were far in excess of the evils. To the existence of a weekly paper published in our State we trace no little of the advance and improvement everywhere to be seen in church matters during the last twenty years.

In September, 1875, T. H. Perrin and the writer began the publication of *Our Faith*, a monthly, which was received with much favor, and, after continuing a year and seven months, was disposed of to the *St. Louis Observer*. It paid its way from the first issue, and rendered the proprietors some profit besides

As the writer was connected with all these interests, he wishes to record here his gratitude to Almighty God for his help and guidance under all these mighty responsibilities, and especially for his constant blessings during the dark and stormy scenes of the "cruel war" in which our unfortunate country was plunged. *How* we managed to publish a weekly paper—begin it without a dollar of capital, with no visible aid a day in advance, under such fearful circumstances—and carry it on successfully during all the war, never lose an issue, never have a note go to protest nor a friend to lose a dollar on our account, with a mission church, fearfully in debt, on hands at the same time, which paid but $300 or $400 to the preacher for his support— we say, *how* all this was done the reader will know as much about as the writer. We can only record that we believe in our inmost soul that "God was our helper;" and to his blessed name be all the honor forever and ever. Wonderful to record!

the paper steadily increased in patronage to the day we separated from it; and had not our poverty and the debt incurred to start it made it indispensable to sell, in order to pay the debt, we might, perhaps, have still been connected with its interests.

# CHAPTER XI.

### EDUCATIONAL EFFORTS.

THERE is no subject on which Cumberland Presbyterians have been less understood than on the subject of education. For many years it was currently reported and believed, by a large number, that our people were not only destitute of common intelligence, but that they were in favor of an illiterate ministry. I am sorry to have cause for saying that many in the "mother church," for the first twenty-five years of our denominational existence, gave strength to this unjust charge, by repeatedly publishing, in their books and papers, that the main cause for the separation and organization of the Cumberland Presbyterian Church was that they did not believe in an educated ministry, and especially in a ministry classically educated. There never was a shadow of truth in this charge. On the contrary, it is the firm conviction of the writer that no denomination of people on the continent have given stronger evidence of their love for, and high appreciation of, a thoroughly educated ministry than has our infant Church. Of course, in making up our judgment in the case we must take into the account all the circumstances of their condition: their "deep poverty," their paucity in numbers, their lack of the means and facilities to promote education, the "waste howling wilderness" which surrounded them on all sides for hundreds of miles, inhabited mostly by wild beasts and wild Indians—the latter more to be feared than the beasts of prey.

At the organization, or rather re-organization, of Cumberland Presbytery in 1810, there was not, west of the Alleghanies, a single school under the control of either Church or State which would now be deemed worthy the name of a college. A collegiate education for the ministry, as required by the old Westminster, was an impossibility. And yet we find our fathers consulting about a college to educate the rising ministry, among the first things to which they turned their attention after their organization as a body. Scarcely had Illinois Presbytery been organized before we find some steps taken to aid candidates for the ministry in securing an education, by a kind of "school of the prophets" organized on a small scale. Rev. David W. McLin—who, perhaps more than any other man, gave shape to the early operations of the Church in Illinois—founded a school at his own house or in his neighborhood, where he taught candidates for the ministry. Rev. J. M. Miller, pastor of the church at Enfield, where Mr. McLin first settled and taught this school, says: "In early times candidates for the ministry boarded free with families here and were taught by Rev. D. W. McLin. Among these candidates I recollect J. S. Alexander, B. Bruce, A. F. Trousdale, N. G. Furguson, and, I believe, Neill Johnson; perhaps Joel Knight, too." Mr. Miller adds: "I know that Neill Johnson, a young minister, dressed himself for marriage at my father's house (James Miller), and married Miss Rolofson." Elder Alexander Stewart, of Albion, Ill., who is one of the oldest elders now living in the State, says in a letter to the writer, that "in 1824 James Alexander, Duke Furguson, Nimrod Furguson, and Alexander Trousdale studied theology under Mr. McLin that winter." For several years this was all the chance for a school—to go to a select school in Winter, and to study theology from the Bible while on the circuit, with the Holy Spirit as teacher, or with some of the older ministers, while active operations in preaching and campmeetings were kept up.

Rev. J. M. Miller informs us that "Ewing Seminary, founded in 1843 under the care of Illinois Presbytery, and afterwards transferred to Illinois Synod, was in active operation but a short time." *Where* this school was located he does not say. But he adds that "Enfield High School, located at Enfield, Ill., chartered in 1873, under the care of Ewing Presbytery, is in successful operation near the close of its fourth year. (The year is now closed.—ED.) Principal, Prof. J. Turrentine; building, brick; value, about $6,000." There have been also several other Seminaries or High Schools started and operated by our people at different periods and in different places. Since the writer has been a resident of the State (from 1855), he remembers LeRoy Seminary, at LeRoy; Stouts Grove Seminary, Stouts Grove; Cherry Grove Seminary, at Abingdon; Mt. Zion Seminary, at Mt. Zion; Sullivan Academy, Sullivan; and Union College, at Virginia. None of these are in operation now, except the High School at Enfield. All these seminaries and the college did a good work in their time. But, where the "free school" system becomes so perfect and general over the State, select schools, where tuition has to be paid and no endowment is secured, cannot long hold out in competition with the common schools of the country. LeRoy and Stouts Grove Seminaries were both under the supervision of McAdow Presbytery. Stouts Grove was, perhaps, the first Seminary established by our people in the State. We append the following from Rev. J. R. Lowrance, who was for years pastor of the church at Stouts Grove, as a reliable statement concerning these schools :

### STOUTS GROVE SEMINARY.

"In 1849 the citizens of Stouts Grove met and resolved to establish a school of high order, to be under the care of Mackinaw Presbytery, the citizens appointing five trustees and the Presbytery six. These trustees, so appointed, met in the church in Stouts Grove on Friday, 6 o'clock P. M., before the second Sabbath in November, 1849. Thus this school was established, and continued for about three years, having at one time about seventy students. Of this company of the youth of that school, some are now filling high places in the Church and State. The present Governor of Illinois, Hon. Shelby M. Cullom, was one of those pupils. This school was under the management of Rev. Cyrus Haynes. Seven of these students were candidates for the ministry.

### LEROY SEMINARY.

"This school was a continuation of Stouts Grove Seminary, and was located there in the year 1852, and a charter was obtained in the Winter of 1853; but after a few years of toil and usefulness it closed out and ceased to exist."

### SULLIVAN ACADEMY,

at Sullivan, the county seat of Moultrie county, was founded by Rev. James Freeland, a graduate of Cumberland University. He was a young man of great promise, and, in addition to preaching every Sabbath, established this Seminary at Sullivan in the Fall of 1851, which he carried on successfully for five or six years. He died April 27, 1856, greatly lamented by all who knew him. The Academy, after his death, fell under influences not favorable to our denomination. But it existed long enough to do a valuable work.

### UNION COLLEGE.

In the Spring of 1851 Sangamon Presbytery, in session at Concord church, Menard county, took steps towards founding an academy or seminary of learning, to be under the control of the Presbytery. They appointed trustees, who were "empowered to receive subscriptions, select the location and erect the house, as soon as they may receive funds sufficient, and do all other matters and things pertaining thereto; and report to the Fall session of this Presbytery of their doings."—Minutes of Sangamon Presbytery, page 269. These trustees were John M. Berry, N. H. Downing, A. H. Goodpasture, Elihu Bone, and David Blair. At the Fall session two more trustees were elected, and those before appointed reported progress: that a sight had been selected at Virginia, Ill., and a contract for material for a suitable house had been made. In short, this institution was started and continued with encouraging results for some years. It was then transferred by Sangamon Presbytery to Sangamon Synod, and from this body transferred again to Sangamon and Illinois Synods, each Synod having an equal voice in its control, and also being equal in its responsibilities. A new charter was obtained from the Legislature, and henceforth it was called no longer a seminary, but Union College. For a time its prospects seemed encouraging; but on account of misunderstandings about the conditions of the last transfer, and perhaps other things, its success was brief. It lived, however, long enough to do a good work. Some able teachers were engaged in its behalf. At one time Rev. S. T. Anderson, late missionary to Trinidad, West Indies, taught there; and, although it was discontinued and has long since ceased to be used for an institution of learning, it is believed that it, and similar efforts in one or two other places, laid the foundation for the final grand success realized in Lincoln University.

All seeming failures are not failures, after all. An institution of learning is never a failure. Its influences for good can never be unavailing. They are lasting as eternity. The brick, stone or wood comprising the building may decay and crumble to atoms; misfortunes may involve the institution in hopeless confusion and certain death; but the influence it has exerted, during even a short existence, it is as impossible to blot out as it is to annihilate the sun. At the time, and under the circumstances, the effort to establish Union College was a noble one, the good effects of which, we doubt not, will be seen in eternity, although it did not accomplish all its friends hoped it would. If we mistake not, after paying the debts of the College, the money remaining was given to the University. So the object is still being attained for which the means were originally contributed, they having been transferred to a different locality.

We append the following brief notice of

### MOUNT ZION SEMINARY

from the pen of Rev. N. M. Baker, the present worthy Stated Clerk of Decatur Presbytery:

"Mount Zion Seminary was located at Mount Zion, within the bounds of this (Decatur) Presbytery. It was erected by the subscriptions of private parties, and owned and controlled by them as stock holders for several years. It was then tendered to the Presbytery by the stock holders, and was accepted by it at a called session which met at Mt. Zion Jan. 30th, 1865. The Presbytery made several attempts to endow this institution, which were unsuccessful, and it finally declined and is not now in operation, the buildings being used for district school purposes under a lease from the Presbytery. The decline of this school, I think, was occasioned, not by the establishing of Lincoln University, nor by any want of energy in its movement, but by the improvement in the free school system, by which schools of equal grade were established in almost all the villages and towns, thus cutting off its patronage, and really removing the cause for its existence. While it was needed it accomplished a great work, and many yet live and labor in positions of usefulness who will ever bless the public spirit and liberality of its founders."

### LINCOLN UNIVERSITY.

The history of education in Illinois would be incomplete indeed without some mention of Lincoln University. Although not connected with the very early struggles, it has played no insignificant part in the growth and prosperity of our Church in the State. In lieu of something more definite, we quote from the first number of the *Alumni Journal* this sketch, written by the facile pen of Dr. D. M. Harris:

"Great calamities are often attended by great blessings. 'It is an ill wind that blows nobody good,' is an adage often verified in the affairs of men. During our great national struggle the causes that led to the origin of Lincoln University had their beginning. In those dark and fearful days of our national and political history, the Cumberland Presbyterian Church in the Northwest passed through a struggle for existence. The fearful tide of war that swept over the South threatened to overthrow and destroy every enterprise of the Church. Our colleges and seminaries suffered in a marked and peculiar manner, resulting in the entire suspension of all active operations. In the Western States the denomination had planted many churches, which were suffering for the want of ministers to supply them. The schools of the Church were unable to meet the demand. Then it was that true and noble men began to reflect upon the future of the Church and her ministry, and tremblingly to enquire, 'What shall we do?' It seemed almost madness to talk of founding and endowing a University. The minds, hearts, lives, and riches of men were staked upon the issues of the war. But genuine faith mocks at failure and laughs at impossibilities. Men were ready to embark in an enterprise of great moment, with omens unpropitious and fates contrary. Unfaltering trust in the promises of Providence and a firm belief in the mission of the Church were all that rendered the project a possibility, at such an unpropitious time.

"As far as we are able to learn, the proposition to establish a college for the Church in the Northwest originated in the Synod of Indiana. Revs. James Ritchey and Elam McCord were among the first to advocate the enterprise. There were such men in the Synod as Azel Freeman, D. D., Revs. A. J. Strain and Ephraim Hall, who heartily endorsed the measure. In Illinois, the proposition was hailed with enthusiasm. Among the most earnest workers in the State were Revs. J. R. Brown, D. D., S. Richards, D. D., A. J. McGlumphy, D. D., J. C. Smith, J. C. Van Patten, J. H. Hughey, James White, J. G. White, and, above all, J. B. Logan. In Iowa, Revs. J. R. Lowrance and W. F. Baird stood among the foremost of all. There were many laymen who did excellent service in and out of the Synods.

"When the Synods had fully decided to begin the work, a commission of five persons (one from each Synod) was appointed to receive bids for the location of the institution, with power to select the place. The places competing for the location of the institution were Newburgh, Ind.; Mt. Zion, Cherry Grove, Virginia, and Lincoln, Ill. The following communication from the citizens of Lincoln will be of interest to many:

" 'LINCOLN, ILL., October 18th, 1864.

" 'WHEREAS, The Cumberland Presbyterian Church purpose founding a college in the State of Illinois; and, for the purpose of securing the location of said college at the town of Lincoln, Logan county, Illinois, or within one-half a mile of the corporate limits of the same, we, the undersigned, severally promise and agree to pay to John Howser, George W. Edgar, George H. Campbell, Benjamin H. Brainerd and William P. Randolph, all citizens of Logan county, Ill., the sum set opposite our respective names, to be applied in the erection of said college buildings, PROVIDED said college is located as aforesaid, at or near the town of Lincoln, Logan county, Illinois.'

"Then follows a long list of names, with a subscription amounting to about $25,000, which was subsequently considerably increased.

"The communication then adds:

" 'The young and flourishing town of Lincoln, as well as the young and prosperous county of Logan, having as yet no institution of learning of a high grade, would hail with joy and pride the location of your college at this place, and would take a lively interest, as well as a commendable pride, in fostering and endowing the institution; and the college would, perhaps, meet with less opposition and competition here than at any other point.

GEO. H. CAMPBELL,<br>
ROBT. B. LATHAM, } Committee.'<br>
JAMES WHITE,

"It is far from our intention to neglect mentioning any whose services deserve attention. There are no doubt many whose names are here not recorded, whose zeal and efficiency were unsurpassed. It is our misfortune to know but little of the first efforts of the friends of the college.

"The citizens of Lincoln have done all that they obligated themselves to do; and we feel sure that the sacrifices made by such generous men as Judge G. H. Campbell, George W. Edgar and Abram Mayfield, in superintending the erection of the building and in securing its speedy completion, cannot be too highly appreciated by the friends abroad.

"The first Faculty consisted of Rev. Azel Freeman, D.D., President; Rev. A. J. McGlumphy, A. M., Vice President and Professor of Mathematics; and Joseph F. Latimer, A. B., Professor of Natural Science. These earnest Christian teachers are entitled to great credit for the high and honorable code of morality and academical character of the students of Lincoln University. To them was committed the important duty of stamping individuality upon the institution. How nobly they accomplished their task, is known to all who have any knowledge of the character and standing of the students of the University.

"To no man more than to Dr. Freeman is the University indebted for the high sense of honor that prevails among the students. His generous, broad and liberal spirit; his earnest, constant and childlike simplicity; his pure, deep and zealous piety; and his profound and comprehensive learning, won for him the love and esteem of all his pupils and co-laborers. His earnest and deep Christian character so thoroughly impressed itself upon the individuality of the college, that many a decade will not efface it. After serving the institution for four years to the entire satisfaction of all who were officially connected with it, he retired from the Presidency honored and loved.

"Rev. J. C. Bowdon, D. D., became his successor. During Dr. Bowdon's administration no new policy of any importance was inaugurated. He found the institution under a good, substantial organization, and was content to work out the plans already in existence. His personal suavity and unbounded generosity made him a universal favorite. He had a heart and a hand for every good cause. He possessed a liberal and general culture that placed him among the foremost scholars of the Church. His uniform kindness, his popular address and his sparkling wit, won for the University many ardent admirers and liberal patrons. A frail body, urged on by a too willing spirit, soon yielded to the power of disease; and one of the most generous, genial souls that ever animated human dust threw aside its mortality, and joined the ranks of the blessed.

"Rev. A. J. McGlumphy, D. D., was elected to fill the vacancy occasioned by the death of President Bowdon. Dr. McGlumphy's eminent success as a teacher, and his strict adherence to the conservative policy of our older and more renowned colleges, guarantee his fitness for the responsible station he fills. His positive and vigorous mode of government; his firm and uncompromising devotion to curriculum, and his fixed determination to maintain a high standard of scholarship, bespeak for him the confidence and the undivided support of the Church. Under his administration, the Church may confidently look for the speedy removal of any imperfections that may exist either in discipline or scholarship. It is not said to the disparagement of Dr. McGlumphy's predecessors that the college breathes a more healthful air and exhibits a more vigorous spirit now than ever before."

It is to be regretted that the unexpected death of the Editor prevents the correction of any inaccuracies which may be in the foregoing statement. Doubtless they exist. There is good reason for thinking that the scheme of founding an institution of learning in this State for the education of our rising ministry originated with the Editor himself. It is certain that, when he published the *Western Cumberland Presbyterian*, the subject was discussed by him editorially, and its importance set forth. Rev. J. R. Brown, D. D,, then in charge of Cherry Grove Seminary at Abingdon, Ill., also wrote upon the subject in that paper under the signature "Omicron;" and to these two men, perhaps more than to any others, is the Church indebted for the origin of the proposition to establish Lincoln University.

A suitable financial statement is also lacking. It may be well to say, however, that the University is in a sound financial condition, and has an endowment of about $100,000. It has an able and faithful corps of instructors, registers a goodly number of students, and has few superiors in point of scholarship in the West.

# CHAPTER XII.

## MOTHERS IN ISRAEL.

To Rev. Neill Johnson we are indebted for the following sketch of

### OLD MOTHER BARNES.

"I first became acquainted with this lady about the year 1828. She was the wife of a Revolutionary soldier, and was brought into the Church at an advanced age. She and her aged companion were poor, and lived mainly on a pension of $8 per month, which he drew for his Revolutionary services. Unfortunately, like many of those noble old patriots, he was considerably intemperate. Aside from this, he was a patriotic, dignified old man. They lived six miles from the place of my regular appointment, and, notwithstanding her age, she was always present at my appointments, performing the journey on foot. At a certain time she came to me with a silver dollar. 'Here,' says she, 'Bro. J., is a dollar. I am sorry I cannot give you more, but it is all I can do at the present.' I was taken considerably by surprise. I said, 'Mother Barnes, excuse me. I am truly thankful to you for your good will, but you need this money far more than I do. Keep it, and lay it out for some of the comforts of this life suitable to your old age.' 'No, Bro. J.,' said she, 'I have already received greater comfort from those precious truths that you preach from time to time than any thing this world can afford.' While I still hesitated in taking it from her, she said, 'I shall really feel hurt, and think hard of you, if you do not take it. To this last appeal I had to submit.

"At that day a silver dollar was a greater amount, in many respects, than ten dollars would be to-day, and, considering the person and the circumstance under which it was given, I this day believe that our blessed Savior will reckon it to mother Barnes as being more than the fifties and the hundreds that make such a flourish in the receipts of our Boards. What influence the giving this dollar had upon the giver I am not prepared to say; but the influence it had upon the receiver has never passed away, though it lacks but little of half a century since it took place. It is often felt as follows: Where I am going to preach, Lord, to-day, there are some of thy hungry lambs. I have come entrusted and commanded to feed them. Shall I disappoint them and send them away hungry? The responsibility has so pressed on me that it tended to drive me to a throne of grace for help.

"Dear old sister Barnes has long since passed from her poverty, toils and sorrows to a rich inheritance in her heavenly father's mansion, and perhaps not a half dozen that were once associated with her in the Church militant are this side of the river. Her remains lie, I believe, in the burying ground in Stouts Grove, and perhaps not a stone tells where she lies; but God looks down, and will watch her sleeping dust till he shall bid it rise."

Richard Beard, D. D., sends this sketch:

### MRS. ANN FOSTER.

"Mrs. Ann Foster, wife of Rev. David Foster, was, before her marriage, Miss Ann Beard. She was the daughter of Captain David Beard. Her mother's original name was Isabel Carson. Her father and mother were both Virginians. Captain Beard was an officer in the Revolutionary War, and bore an active part in the battle of Guilford Court House and in the siege of Yorktown. He was, I suppose, a native of Bedford county, in Virginia, as I have learned from the family history that his father lived and died in that county, and I have never been able to trace the lineage of the family farther up.

"Captain Beard was a member of the Presbyterian Church, and connected in Virginia with one of the congregations of Rev. David Rice, who afterwards became the father of Presbyterianism in Kentucky. The subject of this sketch was born in Virginia, and was doubtless baptized by Mr. Rice. Sometime about 1784 her father moved from Virginia to the West, and made his final settlement in Sumner county, Tennessee, about six miles from where Gallatin now stands. He and his family, as far as they were professors of religion, connected themselves with Shiloh congregation, which was successively under the pastoral care of Revs. Thomas B., Craighead, William McGee, and William Hodge. Shiloh became historical in the old revival of 1800. That work reached the congregation early in the century, and the pastor, Mr. Hodge, became one of its most active supporters. In that revival Captain Beard himself, after a long and terrible experience (in the course of which, from despair of his spiritual condition's ever being improved, he was often driven to the borders of suicide), made a second profession of religion. The daughter, Ann, soon became an earnest inquirer for what had come to seem *the new way*. She appears, as tradition represents her, to have been a very thoughtful young woman. She was hard to satisfy with her spiritual condition, and had a long and doubtful struggle for such evidences of a spiritual renewal as she desired. The writer recollects to have heard her say, perhaps more than once, that at one of the camp-meetings at Shiloh, in the early part of the revival, Mr. Craighead conversed with her frequently, and tried to convince her that she was a Christian. Her own account of the matter was, that she knew well enough that she was not. The good man was, no doubt, honest, and many persons would have accepted his decision, and acted upon it; but she was too earnest to be satisfied with a shadow. In process of time, however, she passed out from under the cloud. It was a real transition—a conversion characteristic of the times. There never was a more earnest Christian woman. Her influence began to be felt immediately, and, considering her social position, it was evidently to a wide extent.

"Her marriage to Mr. Foster was a marriage, as I used to hear it mentioned in our family, based upon Christian principles. I have heard old Mr. Foster, too, the father of David Foster, speak of it. He was one of the best of old men. David Foster had just fairly entered the ministry. He thought of marrying, but times were stormy. He had taken a stand with what became the Cumberland Presbyterian Church. But their prospects were very dark. There were pressing calls for preaching, but the preachers had no encouragement. He consulted his father on the subject of his thoughts. The good old man admitted the darkness of the prospect, was not sure that a young preacher, under such circumstances, ought to marry, but decided, if his mind was to marry, that there was one woman who would suit him, and that to a marriage with her he could give his cordial consent. That woman was the subject of this sketch. The families were neighbors, and well acquainted. They were in mutual sympathy on the subject of religion. It was a "marriage in the Lord." Rev. William Hodge was the officiating minister. It was the first marriage that the writer ever witnessed. It occurred far back in his early boyhood. Mr. Foster bought a little farm and settled near his father in Sumner county.

"In the course of a very few years—two or three, perhaps—he was called to the charge of some congregations in Wilson county. He moved and settled in Suggs' Creek congregation. Here the real work of his life and of that of his wife commenced. He preached to three congregations about nine months in the year, and the other three months were spent, according to the custom of the times, in attending camp-meetings. These often took him far from home, and sometimes three or four weeks in succession. The wife had the burden of the home to bear. She was always frail, yet she administered the affairs of her household with a patience, an earnestness and a heroism which deserved the crown of martyrdom. I was accustomed occasionally to spend months in succession at her house, and I have no recollection of ever seeing a hired female domestic in her family. Indeed, for some years her house was a sort of second home, and she was a sort of second mother to me. I was, therefore, well acquainted with her burdens, and the manner in which she bore them. At one time, in the latter part of 1824, I was in an almost hopeless state of health, and retreated to Mr. Foster's for rest and recuperation for a while. In the time under medical direction, a portion of calomel brought on one of the worst cases of salivation that I ever witnessed. My good aunt was my nurse, and she was indefatigable in her attentions. By day or by night, when necessary, she was at my bed-side, ready to afford what relief was possible. All this, too, was in addition to her own household cares.

"After Mr. Foster moved to Illinois, I think I never saw his wife. In addition to his removal my own line of life changed. From being a traveling preacher I was driven, by a failure of health, to the school room, and of course was very much confined. Of her latter days, therefore, I knew nothing. I have no doubt, however, that they were the days of an earnest Christian woman. It could scarcely have been otherwise.

"There was one feature in Mrs. Foster's religious life which was too prominent and too distinctly marked to be overlooked in a sketch like this. She sometimes, as long as I knew her, under the influence of high religious excitement, would break silence, and not merely shout aloud, but exhort her friends and by-standers. Her exhortations, too, were not the mere incoherent ravings of an unbridled imagination, but they were conceived and expressed with an astonishing degree of correctness. Ordinarily she was a woman of few words, and her intelligence was not above what might have been expected in a woman raised as she was, and having the limited advantages in future life which she had; but on the occasions of which I speak she always transcended herself. The people sometimes said that when she threw aside her respect for the rules of order she was a better preacher than her husband. The hearer involuntarily lost sight of the irregularity of the proceeding under the influence of tender and powerful appeals in behalf of the truth. Her case, however, was not an isolated one. We had other mothers in Israel who threw themselves as earnestly and as decidely into the great work of the times. We witnessed without offense these outpourings of earnest hearts, which, we were satisfied from other sources, were right in the sight of God. I suppose myself that the Savior accepted them upon the same principle that led him to the acceptance of the hosannahs of the multitude at the descent of the Mount of Olives, when he replied to the murmuring Pharisees, 'I tell you that if these should hold their peace, the *very stones would immediately cry out.*'

"Let it not be said that I have become an advocate for irregularities and disorders in the house of God. I acknowledge the authority of Paul in its fullest sense. We all acknowledge the necessity and authority of general rules; yet it sometimes happens that the very interest and expressiveness of a proceeding arise, in a great measure, from its departure from all rules, and from its overlooking all precedents. I place the proceedings which I have mentioned in this category.

"It affords me great satisfaction to be thus able, even at this late day, to render a tribute, however imperfect, to the memory of one of the best Christian women that I ever knew, and of one of the best and sincerest friends of my youth and early manhood."

We are indebted to the kindness of Rev. P. H. Crider for this sketch of

### MRS. MARY ANN WILSON.

"Mary Ann Wilson was born January 30th, 1788. She removed from East Tennessee to Macon county, Illinois, about the year 1830. Mrs. Wilson was an exemplary and faithful Christian, and a devoted friend and member of the Cumberland Presbyterian Church to the day of her death. I am told by her daughter, Mrs. Nancy Wilson, who lives near Decatur, that she, during the latter years of her life, could not be satisfied without going back occasionally to attend meeting at Mt. Zion, her early church home, although she lived several miles away. An excellent sister living in Mt Zion tells me that Aunt 'Polly Wilson,' as she was generally known, told her, a short time before her death, that she had never failed to attend the camp and protracted meetings at Mt. Zion for forty-one years, except in one single instance. This, of course, embraced every year in the history of the church from its organization.

"The following are the names of her children: 1. Thos. B. Wilson, D. D., was born July 26th, 1807, and died July, 1873. He went from Tennessee to Alabama, and from there to Texas. He was pastor of the Cumberland Presbyterian church at Marshall, Texas, at the time of his death. 2. Alexander McClure Wilson was born May 6th, 1809, and is still living and preaching in Kansas. 3. Eliza D. Wilson was born April 15th, 1811, and died Sept. 13, 1815. 4. Katherine Wilson was born in 1816, and died Jan. 7, 1855. 5. Nancy Wilson, now living. 6. John A. Wilson was born Jan. 9, 1819, and died Dec. 18, 1821. 7. James J. Wilson was born November 12, 1822, and died April 28th, 1854, at Princeton, Ky., only a few weeks before he was to graduate in Cumberland College. One son died in infancy, and all the other sons became ministers of the gospel.

"This excellent mother in Israel, Mrs. Mary Ann Wilson, died September 17, 1872, being 84 years, 7 months and 17 days old. Her remains were deposited by the side of her husband in the cemetery at Mt. Zion. While we say, Peace to her ashes, her memory will not be forgotten by many of the present generation living in the community of Mt. Zion. She formerly lived at Mt. Zion, and the ground on which the church, the cemetery, and the academy building were located, was obtained from the tract of land that belonged to her husband, but is now owned by S. K. Smith."

## CHAPTER XIII.

### BIOGRAPHICAL.

Rev. W. W. M. Barber, of Windsor, Ill., has furnished this sketch of his father,

#### REV. JOHN BARBER, SEN.

"Rev. John Barber, Sen., was born in Lincoln county, N. C., Jan. 15th, 1780. His father was a Colonel in the Revolutionary War. His name was also John, which appeared to be a favorite name, as it has been perpetuated in the family. His mother's name is not now remembered. Mr. Barber's parents were members of the Presbyterian Church, and he was raised up in that faith and became a member in his 16th year. He was the subject of the revival that began in North Carolina in 1796, and culminated so powerfully in 1800, out of which the Cumberland Presbyterian Church emanated.

"In early life he became greatly exercised for the salvation of sinners; was active in religious meetings, and would frequently give public exhortations. He was thus early in life impressed with reference to preaching the gospel. His way seemed hedged up in the Presbyterian Church from two considerations: First, his education was limited, though he possessed some advantages over many others. He had a good common education, and when only sixteen years of age was employed in teaching school. While he made no pretention to much education, yet he had given some attention to Latin, besides the common branches of the day. He also had serious objections to the doctrine of fatality, as taught in the Westminster Confession, and, being poor, he did not feel that he could obtain that amount of education that would commend him to the Presbyterian pulpit. He settled down, and, when quite young, married. But this did not relieve his mind on the subject of preaching the gospel. He tried to stifle his feelings; and in this state of mind in the year 1815 he came to Illinois, and settled in Madison county, near Edwardsville, the county seat. In the neighborhood where he settled there were, including himself, three elders, and about twenty members of the Presbyterian Church. Mr. Barber had been ordained an elder before leaving North Carolina. His impressions to preach became more intense, and, finding that the Cumberland Presbyterian Confession of Faith only made a good English education indispensable in order to enter the ministry, he, in the forty-fourth year of his age, was sent as a representative from Mt. Gilead society to the second session of Illinois Presbytery, which met at New Salem, Gallatin county, Ill., Oct. 14th, 1823, at which meeting he became a candidate for the ministry. Mr. Barber was licensed to preach the gospel as a probationer for the holy ministry April 9th, 1824, at the house of James Johnson, Mt. Gilead, Bond county, Ill. He was ordained to the whole work of the gospel ministry at the house of Joseph Robison, Madison county, Ill., Thursday after the first Tuesday in April, 1826, having been a licentiate two years. Mr. Barber was respected as a good Christian man and citizen, a man of considerable reading and extensive knowledge. He had been called by his fellow citizens to fill civil offices, and for a number of years filled the office of Justice of the Peace.

"Possessing a strong mind and having some ambition, after joining Presbytery he made rapid progress in scientific pursuits, so that in six months after his reception as a candidate he was licensed to preach, and went heartily into the work. From his journal we learn that he had occasional seasons of gloom and discouragements. The remarks, after telling where and from what text he had preached, were very dissimilar from each other on different occasions. At one time he said, 'I had light, liberty, power; people feeling;' at another time he said, 'I had no light, no liberty, no heat, no power; dull myself; people dull.' At one time large congregations, again few or none, were present. At one time he was much encouraged; at other times discouraged, and tempted to quit preaching.

"What he received for preaching, and from whom and when, were faithfully kept in his journal. His report to the Fall Presbytery of 1830 will show something of the work performed and the amount received. He says, 'I would beg leave to report to Presbytery, that I have preached one hundred and two sermons since last Presbytery; have baptized one adult and twelve infants. I have organized one church with thirteen members, which were received by letter, and have received four or five members by experience in the bounds of my particular labors. I have spent one hundred and eight week days, including the time spent in attending the judicatures of the Church, and have received $4.50, $3 of which were given by the ministers to defray my expenses to the General Assembly. I have attended six camp-meetings and twelve two-days' meetings. At our camp-meetings, and other places where I have labored, I have an account of fifty-three who have professed religion. The calls for ministerial labor are increasing, and many of them come from persons who are members of our Church, but are now living far from where they can hear a Cumberland Presbyterian voice. I cannot see how these calls are to be met, unless we have itinerant preachers. But preachers cannot live on the wind, and there appears to be but little prospect of any measures by which they can be supported. There is a fault among Cumberland Presbyterians on this subject, and if there is not something done soon, if the gospel does not sink, Cumberland Presbyterianism must and will sink. But I desist.'

"In a report prior to this the amount of work was something similar, the amount received was one dollar, and the distance traveled about eighty miles per month. About this time was a gloomy period in the history of the Cumberland Presbyterian Church, and one who left it boasted that there would be a general stampede. While there were inducements held out, none but poor Ogden left with him (Smith).

"Mr. Barber was a strong advocate of temperance, and was the first in his neighborhood to dispense with the use of liquor at meetings for work. When he invited his friends to assist him in his work, he informed them that he was not going to furnish ardent spirits on the occasion. Many said they would not help; but they had respect for his conscientious convictions, and he experienced no difficulty. By his boldness he set an example that was followed by his neighbors. He often lectured on temperance, and made overtures in private to such as he considered in danger of being injured by strong drink. Once, three or four young men, that he had admonished to quit drinking, agreed that they would quit if he would quit the use of tobacco. On mature and prayerful reflection he accepted the proposition. In a few months afterwards they inquired how he got along. He confessed that it went hard with him to do without his tobacco. They proposed to mutually withdraw from their pledges. He declined their offer. Those young men lived orderly and sober lives.

"Mr. Barber had an ardent love for souls, and up to within a short period before his death he traveled some forty miles or more to visit churches that he had planted. His last visit to Madison county, where he first settled, was attended with difficulty, from an affliction in his limbs affecting him to such an extent that he sometimes sat and preached. He preached six times during this visit, and spoke of it with

tears as his last visit. A short time after this, in a letter to his son, Dr. Barber, he says: 'I have kept up my regular appointments, but feel like giving them up. I am always extremely tired on Sabbath evenings.   *   *   *   *
I look forward with joy to that sweet rest which is just before me, and will be given me, when the toils of life are over, by my blessed Redeemer. These thoughts cheer my soul often in view of my final end. The thought of that rest makes me feel that no affliction here is worth a thought when compared with the glory that shall be revealed; and the thought of winning souls to Jesus seems more than all my toils. I have frequently thought that, if I had my choice when and where to die, it would be to die in the pulpit entreating sinners to come to Jesus. But I will leave the when, and the where, and the how I shall bid the world adieu, to him who has bought me with his own blood, and who, I hope, will be glorified in me, whether by life or death. As long as I can speak intelligently, and can reach the assembly who meet to worship God, I will endeavor to preach Jesus and him crucified, the way, the truth and the life.'

"In another letter to the same, he alludes to the infirmities of old age in strains of a true Christian philosopher. He says: 'I suppose that you feel by this time somewhat as I did before I received yours of the 19th of December: that I am either dead, sick, careless, lazy, busy, or something else. The first two and the last of the above charges have not befallen me yet, but the other two, I fear, stick as close as the skin. You will doubtless perceive by my awkward letters that the old fingers are beginning to threaten disobedience, and if they refuse partial or total obedience, I have no remedy. All the old joints seem to threaten the same, and if they combine they will certainly conquer, for the last seventy-four years' wear and tear will much facilitate the conquest. But what will be conquered? Blood, bones, sinews, flesh and nerves are not me. Life—what is it?

where is it? 'T is not in the head and heart alone, but it is in the end of every finger and toe, and every other part of my system; and yet I cannot fully describe or understand it. With the Psalmist I must exclaim: I am fearfully and wonderfully made.'—Ps. clix. 14.

"Mr. Barber was married four times—twice before leaving North Carolina and twice in Illinois. He had four children by his first wife and four by the last. Of the first family all are dead. Each, however, lived to have a family of his own.

"The last sermon Mr. Barber preached was at old Mount Pleasant church, about six weeks previous to his death. The text was Romans iii. 20. He died Sept. 19, 1855, in his 76th year. He is buried in Bear Creek graveyard, Montgomery county, Ill."

It was our privilege to see Mr. Barber and hear him preach several times. He was a man of extraordinary strength of mind, and had the happy faculty of stating his views clearly and in few words. We visited him and passed a night with him during his last sickness. He was calm and resigned, and looking out momentarily for the Master to call for him. He was unusually beloved, and his death greatly lamented.

### REV. DAVID WILSON M'LIN.

No man connected with the Cumberland Presbyterian Church in Illinois, all things considered, acted the part which this father did in establishing the Church on Illinois soil. It is strange, and sad, too, that a fitting tribute to his memory has not been long since published. We feel that the *data* now within reach is so defective, that it is impossible to do justice to the self-sacrificing toil of this indomitable and successful minister of Jesus. It was not our privilege to meet with him, but, what is perhaps better, we have met with his mighty influence, or rather the influence of our holy religion through his instrumentality, over all our Church territory in Illinois. Everywhere we meet the saving influence of his life and noble character. Whether we traverse the country and talk with the "old settlers," or read the records of Presbyteries and Synods, the name of D. W. McLin stands pre-eminent over all others. We are, therefore, glad of the privilege to do at least a little toward redeeming from oblivion a character and life that ought to be ever held sacred by all Cumberland Presbyterians. The following touching letter from his youngest daughter in Sherman, Texas, will be read with interest:

"I, being the youngest of the family, have no recollection of ever seeing my father, and can only very indistinctly remember my mother; but I do revere and love their names, and feel to ask the blessing of God upon any one who may wish to perpetuate the memory of my sainted father. I will give a few items in reference to his early history, which may be of some importance. Having lived the greater part of my life away from my older sisters and brothers, I have had but little chance to know much of my parents' history.

"My father, David Wilson McLin, was born in North Carolina, December 24th, 1785. He was of Scotch-Irish descent. His parents, James and Catherine McLin, moved from North Carolina to Middle Tennessee when he was quite young. They were of the Presbyterian faith. Father was a convert of the revival of 1800. His early education, I think, was limited, but, from what I have been told, he was a life student. He learned the tailor's trade, and at times during his whole life worked at his trade, when in need of means of support for his family. He often came home after being away preaching for days, and sat up all night working so as to leave the means of subsistence for his family while on another missionary tour, though never neglecting the work of his Master. He was received as a candidate for the ministry March 10, 1810, with Robert Donnell, Robert McCorkle, William Bumpass and William Barnett.

"He remained in Tennessee, riding and preaching, until the division of Cumberland Presbytery; then he joined Logan Presbytery. He preached in Kentucky and Tennessee until sent out as a missionary to Illinois by the Western Missionary Board, of Kentucky, which, from his journal, seems to have been in either 1819 or 1820.

"He was married in 1812 near Hopkinsville, Ky., to Nancy Johnson Porter, daughter of William and Sarah Porter. She was born in Virginia. Her parents moved to Kentucky when she was a child, and settled near Hopkinsville. They were Baptists, but she was not a member of any Church at the time of their marriage. She professed religion soon afterwards and joined the Cumberland Presbyterian Church.

"Father died in Fairfield, Ill., in the Fall of 1836. His disease was dyspepsia. He was a great sufferer a long while before he died, but continued to ride and preach as long as he could sit on his horse, and even after he had to be helped into his saddle from weakness. Just before his death he was making preparations to attend a camp-meeting a few miles from where he lived. He directed all arrangements himself. He had his camp built near the pulpit where he could lie in his bed and enjoy the meeting; but before the time for the meeting came on he grew worse. As death approached, he called his wife and children around him; bade each one an affectionate farewell; advised the older ones in reference to their spiritual interest and their mother's welfare; and then, as might have been expected from the life he had lived, had nothing to do but to calmly fall asleep in Jesus. After his death it was soon ascertained that comparatively nothing was left for the support of his family. The church then bought a place near Fairfield, and gave it to mother, at which she remained till her death, she and her older daughters supporting themselves and the younger children by their own exertions,

"Mother died in the Winter of 1838 of pneumonia. She was an unassuming quiet Christian, of a sweet, gentle disposition. She had a firm and abiding faith in her Savior, and just before her death expressed the belief that her children would be taken care of. Since then we have been a broken, scattered family, yet the Lord of the orphan, whom our parents loved and trusted, has kindly provided for and taken care of each and every one of us. Although we, as a family, have been separated the greater part of our lives, we have the blessed hope of meeting again a happy, unbroken, re-united family in heaven. Only four of us are living now. All the rest have passed through the 'pearly gates,' and are now waiting and watching for those of us left behind."

The following sketch is from our worthy brother, Rev. J. M. Miller, pastor of the church at Enfield, Ill., and who knows whereof he writes:

"In 1815 he was examining committee when John Provine was licensed. He organized Dry Fork church, Middle Tennessee, in the Winter of 1817, where, on October 7th, 1850, his youngest daughter, N. L. McLin, was converted to God. He organized Village church, White county, Ill., in the Fall of 1819; Shiloh church at Burnt Prairie, Nov. 22, 1821; the church at McLeansboro, I think; one near Shawneetown; think he organized Union church in White county; Fairfield and Thom's Prairie churches in Wayne county; and New Pleasant congregation in Gallatin county. About 1829 he moved to Equality, Gallatin county; in 1831 to Burnt Prairie, White county; in 1832 to Fairfield, Wayne county.

"At his death he left a wife, six living daughters and three sons, one son (Finis Ewing) having died July 19, 1825, at the age of 14 months and 25 days. All his children who grew to adult years became members of the Cumberland Presbyterian Church, except, perhaps, one. His fame was not only in all the churches, but in all this country. Mr. A.

Stewart, an aged elder in the Cumberland Presbyterian church in Albion, Ill., soon after his arrival from Scotland, heard him preach in Carmi, White county. While the young Scotchman much admired the speaker and the sermon, he thought it strange to see a minister in a mixed jeans suit! With safety it may be said, the fruit of early labor is not only abundant here, but many, following the tide of emigration, went North and West in this State, and into Iowa, Oregon, Colorado, Kansas, Nebraska, some to Missouri, and some to Texas.

"Rev. McLin was present at the first meeting of Illinois Synod, Mt. Gilead church, Bond county, Ill., Oct. 11, 1832. At that time he, J. S. Alexander, Jesse Pearce and Richard Harris were the members of Illinois Presbytery. Within the same territory are Illinois, Ewing and McLin Presbyteries, with about 30 ordained ministers, and 85 or 90 organized churches. The Presbyterian Church was organized here before Mr. McLin came. Two of my uncles were elders. My father, James Miller, and one uncle, James Mys, became elders in the Cumberland Presbyterian Church, both possessing about equal chances. The growth of the Cumberland Presbyterian Church in the same territory, numerically, is about ten fold greater, indicating zeal, and doctrine that commends itself.

"His mission work, I think, often took him to Shoal Creek, Big Muddy and Silver Creek, as the names became quite familiar to me by hearing him so often speak of them. Travel then was on foot or horseback, and often in the night, to avoid flies.

"The evidence of lasting work might be given at great length. Multitudes will trace their salvation to his instrumentality. His remains rest near Fairfield, Ill."

The following interesting letter is from Rev. J. T. Borah, now of Rienzi, Miss. Mr. Borah was for years a minister in Illinois:

"Rev. David McLin was ordained to the ministry by Cumberland Presbytery in the month of February, 1813, in the neighborhood of Mr. McGhee on Three Forks of Duck River. Some time after his removal to Illinois he and Rev. Nimrod Furguson bought the freedom of a negro preacher. Their object was good. At the time of the purchase, it was believed that the negro might accomplish good as a preacher. But the manumitted slave turned out badly: proved wicked and ungrateful. The former owner exacted rigidly the payment of the purchase money. The conduct of the negro had destroyed all confidence and sympathy. The purchasers had expected assistance; but the whole amount fell upon McLin and Furguson. With that amount to pay, and a large family to support, McLin was pressed for years. Poor Furguson! he fell upon breakers, and finally stranded among the quicksands of infidelity.

"Mr. McLin was a tailor by trade, and had the reputation of being a good one. But he abandoned 'the bench,' entered upon the practice of medicine, and was a successful physician. During all these changes, and under all these trials which fell thick and hard upon him, he faltered not, but was indefatigable in his efforts in the ministry. That great and pressing work seemed ever to absorb his heart and sympathies, notwithstanding the demands upon his energy in supporting his family. He had appointments far and near, in church houses, school houses, and very often at private residences. He possessed the happy art of presenting the beauties of religion, and impressing them upon heart and mind, when out of the pulpit, as well as when in it. Especially among the children did he reign, and his scepter was love. The writer has often sat upon the knees of that sainted man, and listened to the story of a Savior's love, that seemed ever on the lips of the loving, faithful disciple. Whether in the pulpit, at the bedside of the suffering, in the social circle, or amongst romping children, he turned all to account for the advancement of the cause so near his heart. He was a charming preacher, with a clear, ringing voice, pleasant gestures, and eyes that became luminous when excited or enthused with his subject. In stature he was rather low, and somewhat inclined to corpulence; had a bald head, but was exceedingly fine looking, and the neatest man I ever saw. Mr. McLin was once preaching at Shiloh (Burnt Prairie neighborhood), on the old camp-ground. His theme was: 'The Pure River and the Tree of Life.' The effort was truly grand. He was exceedingly brilliant in his descriptions, and carried his hearers onward and upward until it seemed that the preacher stood upon the radiant shore hard by the throne, and the audience were gazing upon the rapt scene. There was a shout sent up by that large concourse, the refrain of which I expect angels took up, and carried to the 'most excellent glory.' The preacher sprang from the pulpit and burst into loud hallelujahs. Many were converted and made happy on that occasion, who, with the grand old preacher, have crossed the dark river and have entered the heavenly city through gates of pearl.

"Dr. McLin preached his last sermon in July or August of the year he died. The meeting was at the residence of Daniel Kinchello in Wayne county, five miles southwest from Fairfield. His text was Isaiah xxviii. 20: 'For the bed is shorter than that a man can stretch himself on it, and the covering narrower than that he can wrap himself in it.' The writer was only a youth, yet the scene will never be forgotten. There stood the old warrior, worn and feeble, trembling under the weight of years and toil, with pale brow, sunken eye, body all emaciated, but the shadow of a man of a few years ago. While elaborating the doctrines of the text he was solemn, pointed, earnest; but when he came to the peroration he was almost fearful in the grandeur of his appeals to the dying sinner without a covering to shelter his suffering soul. It was the last struggle. The work of Rev.

David McLin was done, his warfare ended. He went home, and laid by his armor, calmly and sweetly to die amidst his loved and loving family. His wife and some of his sons and daughters have followed, and are now with him resting under the shadow of a throne white and glorious."

### REV. JOHN M'CUTCHEN BERRY.

The subject of this sketch was born in Virginia, March 22, 1788. Of his parentage and early life but little is now known. His education was necessarily limited. He moved to Tennessee in his fourteenth year, and professed religion among the Cumberland Presbyterians in his twentieth year. His convictions were long and severe, at times bordering on despair. His mind was troubled with the old doctrine of election and reprobation taught in the Westminster Confession. He got to believe that he was eternally reprobated, and that therefore there was no mercy for him. The writer knows from experience something of the terrible anxieties this doctrine can produce when once it gets a lodgment in the mind (For what is here narrated we are mainly indebted to Rev. A. Johnson's letters as published in 1864 in the *Western Cumberland Presbyterian*, of which the writer was then Editor, and to Dr. Beard's "Second Series" of biographical sketches.) When at last the light broke into his soul, he described it as "the sun arising at midnight." Through all his ministerial course he had a great aversion, amounting almost to abhorrence of this terrible doctrine, that man's destiny is fixed from eternity, irrespective of any conditions.

Soon after his conversion he felt it to be his duty to preach the gospel, but strove against the impressions with great resolution. But the impressions followed him, and in order to get away from this duty, and the darkness of mind produced by his rebellion against God, he was greatly tempted to commit suicide, and at one time went out into the darkness to end his existence. Some influence, however, kept him from committing the deed. To drown these feelings he married, and married one who, like himself, was sternly opposed to his trying to be a preacher. He also joined the army in 1812 under Col. Young Ewing. The expedition was against the Indians in Illinois. The regiment marched to Fort Clark, found no Indians, and returned to Kentucky nearly starved for food. Col. Ewing was brother to Rev. Finis Ewing, one of the fathers of the Cumberland Presbyterian Church. Finis Ewing was himself in the regiment as soldier and chaplain. Mr. Berry again entered the army, and was in the celebrated battle of New Orleans, fought on the 8th of January, 1815. It was in this battle, exposed to instant death, with men falling all around him, that Mr. Berry promised God, if spared to return home, he would serve him to the best of his ability in any position he called him. His soul at that time was filled with inexpressible delight and joy.

In 1817 Mr. Berry was received as a candidate under the care of Logan Presbytery. In the Fall of 1819 he was licensed to preach the gospel, and in 1822 he was ordained to the whole work of the gospel ministry. In 1820 he removed to the State of Indiana, where, like all other poor people, he labored on a farm to support his family and preached what he could. Shortly after his ordination he came to Illinois, and was one of the three members who formed the first Presbytery, as recorded elsewhere. He settled in Sangamon county (at that day but sparsely settled), and he was the only preacher of our people in all the northern part of the State. He continued a member of Illinois Presbytery until, in the Spring of 1829, Sangamon Presbytery held its first meeting, and he was one of its five ministers present. He lived and labored in this field for many years with wonderful success. In the latter part of his life he was a member, we think, of Mackinaw Presbytery, and remained so till his death, which occurred in the Winter of 1856 and 1857, at his residence in Clinton, DeWitt county. His last sermon was delivered at old Sugar Creek, in Logan county, some ten miles north of Lincoln, from Rom viii. 28. He died as he had lived: with his armor on, and in the field of battle.

Mr. Berry was a very positive man. His opinions were very decided, and his preaching was bold, frank, unvarnished. The writer first met him in the town of Greenfield, at the session of Sangamon Presbytery in 1854, only a little over two years before his death. He was very impressive as a speaker. His points were made clear and strong, and he was a man of large influence over the entire State. We had the impression that no man of his day, if we may except Rev. Mr. McLin, had as much to do in forming the character and establishing the Cumberland Presbyterian Church in Illinois as had Mr. Berry.

In the latter part of his life he entertained extreme views on the subject of baptism, which crippled his influence with a portion of the Church. In his early ministry he was in the habit of baptizing often by immersion, if the subject preferred this mode. This, indeed, was the common practice thirty years ago. Mr. Berry had a case of this kind. It was a lady. The season was dry, and sufficient water was hard to procure. The baptism was delayed some hours, certain parties having to dam up a little stream so as to accumulate water enough to immerse the body. Mr. Berry felt that he and the entire audience were placed under very embarrassing circumstances. It led him to a careful examination of the subject as to whether God required a mode which, many times, places the subject and administrator under embarrassments like those under which they were laboring. His mind underwent a great revolution on this question, and he came to the firm conviction that immersion is not baptism at all; that all who are immersed are yet unbaptized, and consequently are not in the Church at all—baptism, as he viewed it, being the door into the visible Church. Mr. Berry was not a man to believe strongly in the necessity and importance of a dogma, and not preach it. Accordingly, he preached and argued his new doctrine far and near, producing at the time quite a sensation among the churches of his Presbytery and Synod. So far did he carry his view that he refused to administer the sacrament of the Supper to those who had been immersed, alleging that they were unbaptized, and therefore had no right to partake of the Lord's Supper. About this time he published his book entitled, "The Covenants," in which the doctrine just mentioned is strongly urged. Before the close of his life he seemed to lose sight, somewhat, of this theme, and go back to the themes of his younger days in the ministry; and the excitement over his theory had well nigh died out.

Mr. Berry was very prompt in his attendance upon the judicatories of the Church. He was never absent unless positively hindered by sickness or death, often riding from one hundred to five hundred miles to get there, and that, too, over swollen streams and through mud and almost boundless prairies, many times without any road as a guide to the place of destination. He was a man of great courage and perseverance, of unquestioned integrity and of spotless character. There was one thing which seemed to trouble him more than all else, and that was a son, who became dissipated. Mr. Berry was much from home, and it appears that while not under the immediate eye of his father, the son acquired a taste for strong drink. This, with its attendant evils, gave the parents much anxiety, and even anguish of mind. Dr. Beard relates an incident connected with this son's case, which we think worthy of repeating here. We may here state, that no man could have been more opposed to intemperance, or a stronger advocate of total abstinence from all intoxicating drinks as a beverage, than was Mr. Berry,

His was an uncompromising war upon the enemy at all times. But to the incident: "Abraham Lincoln and Mr. Berry's prodigal son were at one time partners in a little store. It is not so stated, but we should infer from the narrative that they probably sold whisky. Although Mr. Berry could not overcome the obstinacy of his son, he seems to have succeeded with the partner. On one occasion afterward, when Mr. Lincoln had risen to some eminence as a lawyer, a grog shop in a particular neighborhood was exerting a bad influence upon some husbands. The wives of these men united their forces, assailed the establishment, knocked the heads out of the barrels, broke the bottles, and smashed up things generally. The women were prosecuted, and Mr. Lincoln *volunteered* his services in their defense. In the course of a powerful argument upon the evils of the use of, and of the traffic in, ardent spirits, whilst many in the crowded court room were bathed in tears, the speaker turned, and, pointing his bony finger towards Mr. Berry, who was standing near him, said: '*There* is the man who, years ago, was instrumental in convincing me of the evils of traflicing in and using ardent spirits. I am glad that I ever saw him. I am glad that I ever heard his testimony on this terrible subject.'" Several years ago, while traveling in that part of the State in company with another minister, he pointed out to the writer the spot by the roadside where stood the little store referred to by Dr. Beard. Mr. Lincoln is not the only great man in political circles who has received some good influences from the Cumberland Presbyterian Church. Dr. Beard concludes this incident by saying, that Mr. Berry "was more honored that day than he would have been afterwards had he been made Mr. Lincoln's Secretary of State." And so he was.

We did not meet with Mr. Berry but two or three times prior to his death. The last time we saw him was at the meeting of Sangamon Synod the year before his death. He preached on the occasion a good, strong sermon, attended with warmth and energy. The impression made upon the mind of the writer was, that Mr. Berry was a plain, pointed, gospel preacher, seeking no display, desiring no applause from men. And when he was fully enlisted in his subject, he was powerful, and sometimes almost irresistible. He did a great and glorious work, and has gone to his rest and reward.

### REV. ABNER WAYNE LANSDEN.

Mr. Lansden was born in Iredell county, North Carolina, October 1st, 1794; removed with his father's family to Wilson county, Tennessee, in 1807; professed religion in 1820; joined Presbytery with George Donnell and Samuel Aston April 5th, 1821, at old Moriah church, where the family worshiped. He was licensed in the Fall of 1822; ordained in the Spring of 1825. He married Mary M. Gallaher, sister of Revs. James, Allen, and William Gallaher, of the Presbyterian Church, in 1828. He resided in Blount county, Tennessee, till near 1835, when he removed to Sangamon county, Illinois, where he lived thirty-four years. He lived twenty-nine years in one neighborhood, organized and built up the Smyrna congregation. He removed to Saline county, Missouri, in 1869, where his two daughters had gone, and where he breathed his last.

In 1843 his wife died, leaving him with five children, the youngest five and the oldest thirteen years of age. He was married again in 1855 to Miss Sarah L. Lowrance, who survives him. He preached to Smyrna congregation a part, or the whole of his time for twenty-nine years, and after removing to Missouri labored for the most part in the Mount Olivet congregation in New Lebanon Presbytery.

On the last Sabbath in August he preached his last sermon from the text, "What shall I do that I may inherit eternal life?"—Mark x. 17. His sermon was delivered with unusual earnestness. He was a faithful messenger of Christ to dying men for fifty-three years. What a testimony to leave behind!

He lived to see all his children members of the Church, and, we trust, heirs of eternal life.

Mr. Lansden was one of the first ministers the writer remembers to have heard preach. My father's house was a preaching place for the "circuit riders" in East Tennessee for many years. Lansden or George Donnell, I cannot now tell which, came round first, and the other soon followed. He was one of the most efficient instruments in God's hands of establishing the Cumberland Presbyterian Church through all East Tennessee. Many and many a time have I seen him exhort, sing, pray, and labor at camp-meetings till nearly if not quite the break of day. He was a man of whom any Church may well feel proud, for, in his long ministerial life of over fifty-three years, he never had the slightest stain upon his moral character. He ever adorned his calling and brought honor to his Church. In later years I have heard him say the first couple he married was at my father's house, at the close of preaching at one of his monthly appointments. The couple were cousins of mine; and although they were not members of the Church, they named their first-born for him who married them. He left that country when I was but a boy, and when we met, after long years of separation, my heart was too full for utterance.

In all my acquaintance in the Church I never have known a better man. He was a good preacher. His strong points were the doctrines of the gospel, on which he dwelt with great clearness, pathos, and power. His appeals to the unconverted were often almost irresistible. His tender pleadings with them, while tears coursed down his cheeks, were enough to melt, and often under God did melt, hearts of stone. He spent no time in frivolous talking and jesting after service was over. As a father, husband, neighbor, and citizen, he met his responsibilities so that he commanded universal love and esteem. Hundreds, it may be thousands, will rise up and call him blessed as the instrument of their salvation.

Unostentatious, gentle as the dove, he was as firm to his principles as the everlasting hills. He never neglected family religion, was a close observer of the Sabbath, was a total abstainer from all intoxicants. He was faithful to all his Church vows. He was always present at Presbytery and Synod, unless Providentially detained—and that, with him, meant death or serious sickness. He died in great peace at his home in Saline county, Missouri, Sept. 8th, 1875, lacking but twenty-two days of being eighty-two years of age. Shortly before he breathed his last, his two daughters being by his bed, he raised his hand and, pointing upward, said, "It is all light, and no darkness at all." And thus his sun, instead of setting in eternal night, has arisen "no more to go down."

We take pleasure in appending the following letter, written by Rev. Jesse S. Grider to the *Cumberland Presbyterian* shortly after the death of Mr. Lansden. Mr. Grider was then a resident of Illinois, and was traveling in the interests of Lincoln University.

"I was with Bro. Wiley Knowles at his appointment near Auburn, Illinois, on the Sabbath immediately succeeding the announcement in the *Cumberland Presbyterian* of the death of the venerable Abner Lansden. The members of that congregation (Smyrna) had not heard of that sad event, and at the close of the sermon Bro. Knowles arose and said, 'I have a sad announcement to make. Your old pastor, and one long beloved, Father Lansden, is no more.' Immediately the whole congregation broke into tears. The people literally 'lifted up their voices and wept.' An old sister exclaimed, 'My spiritual father has gone to heaven.' An old brother (Jannett) arose from his seat and said, with tears, 'He is not only my spiritual father, but of my whole family. He led us all to Jesus.' I do not remember to have ever witnessed such a scene as this. It has been often said that a monument erected in the affections of a people is more enduring than brass. Father Lansden has certainly one of these heart-monuments erected to his memory.

"I do not think the poet spoke truly when he said, 'The evil that men do lives after them; the good is oft interred with their bones.' Let us prefer the sentiment, 'He, being dead, yet speaketh.'

"Now, Mr. Editor, would you not prefer such a monument as the one erected in the hearts of these people to that of the costliest marble, or the most imperishable brass? This modest, unpretending minister of Christ has left a record behind, in which the most gifted and honored might rejoice.

> " 'Servant of God, well done!
> Rest from thy blest employ;
> The battle fought, the victory won,
> Enter thy Master's joy.' "

As said elsewhere, Mr. Lansden was one of the first, if not the first, preacher I can remember to have heard. After years of separation we met in the Fall of 1853 or 1854 at Mount Zion camp-ground, in Macon county. That was a memorable occasion; for not only was Mr. Lansden present, but his old East Tennessee comrade, Rev. Samuel Aston, who had just come West, and these two met at this meeting for the first time in many years. Mr. Aston took charge of this church, and in a year or two thereafter died, and was buried in the graveyard close by the church.

Mr. Lansden was for several years pastor of old Sugar Creek church, in Sangamon county. During his pastorate there the writer assisted him in a meeting of much interest. His labors extended over a large territory of the State. For a short time, also, he was pastor of Bethany church, in Moultrie county, and may have supplied other churches. But his great work was at old Smyrna. There he lived and labored for a great many years, and left universally beloved.

Mr. Lansden belonged to a generation past. He was remarkable for his simplicity, modesty, and retiring manner, chaste language and dignified demeanor in the pulpit. He never, on any occasion, indulged in light and frivolous conversation in private circles. You could not be with him long without feeling that his conversation was in heaven; that he lived in a holy and pure atmosphere, and that, while he did not seem conscious of it, he occupied a much higher moral plane than the great mass of professed Christians. The one trait of character more prominent than all others was his great humility. He never aspired to be great in the world's estimation. He only wished to be useful. He was willing to take the lowest seat and occupy the humblest place, if only the Master's cause was served. He was rather under the average stature, lean and thin, and possessed of a clear, silvery voice which, once heard for half an hour, could never be forgotten by an attentive listener. Like the most of the fathers of Cumberland Presbyterianism, he had a mind well stored with Bible knowledge, and was well qualified to expound and defend the doctrines of our Church against the extremes of Arminianism and Calvinism. Few men in any Church have lived longer or to a better purpose than did he. One son resides in Cairo, Illinois, another in Kansas; two married daughters and the widow have their homes in Missouri.

### REV. JOEL KNIGHT.

For the historical facts in this sketch we are mainly indebted to the autobiographical sketch which Mr. Knight left for publication at his death, and which was published in consecutive numbers of *Our Faith*. We have, however, gained some additional information from the minutes of Illinois and Vandalia Presbyteries.

Rev. Joel Knight was born at the "Red Banks" (now Henderson) Kentucky, February 22, 1796. His father's name was John Knight, who was born near Baltimore, Md. His mother's maiden name was Ann Roelofson, a native of Pennsylvania. At the time of the birth of Mr. Knight, and for many years after, the Indian wars were frequent and their cruelties horrible. At the time of his birth his oldest brother, Isaac Knight, was a prisoner in the hands of the Indians, where he remained about three years before making his escape. At the age of six years Mr. Knight's father died, leaving his mother a widow with a large family, two children being younger than himself. It is almost needless to say, that at that time and under the circumstances an education was almost out of the question in this Western country. Mr. Knight was what the world would call a self-made, common English scholar. He went to school but little at any time. He speaks as follows of his first religious convictions: "I suppose I was not more than seven years old when I felt that I was a poor sinner, and needed to have my sins pardoned in order to be happy hereafter. I often promised in my own mind, and sometimes publicly, that I would do better and try to become good;.but again I forgot my promises, neglected private prayer, and was as bad as ever. Sometimes I was even more wild; but when at meeting I always paid strict attention to preaching and religious exercises." At the age of eighteen he was married to Miss Martha Bostick, who was a pious member of the Methodist Church. He seems to have lived on in a semi-careless state for several years. In 1818 he attended a Cumberland Presbyterian camp-meeting near where Evansville, Ind., now stands, at which a number of his friends and relatives professed religion. Here he seemed to be greatly troubled on account of his sins, but he says, "I left a poor, distressed, helpless sinner." He wore off somewhat his distress, and engaged in the busy affairs of the world, as usual. Shortly after this he visited Illinois on an exploring trip, and was so pleased with the new country that he determined to remove thither. In the Spring of 1819 he removed to White county, and settled at "Seven Mile Prairie." Here Rev. David W. McLin had previously settled and started a Cumberland

Presbyterian church. Mr. Knight had become firmly convinced that there was a medium ground—which alone was the true ground—between the extremes of Calvinism and the current Arminianism of the country; and when he heard Cumberland Presbyterians preach, their doctrines were just what he believed to be taught in the Holy Scriptures. He became enamored with their theory of the plan of redemption, as alike honoring to God and adapted to the condition of a fallen race. He determined to settle in Mr. McLin's congregation. At this time he had two children. The latter part of the following August a communion meeting was held at Hopewell (now Enfield), where Revs. Wm. Barnett, John Barnett, Wm. Henry, Dr. Johnson and Aaron Shelby were present, besides Mr. McLin. On Monday of this meeting, under a pungent sermon by Rev. John Barnett from John xix. 4, Mr. Knight was brought to see his sins as he had never seen them before. Dr. Johnson preached at night, called the anxious, and Mr. Knight was among those who responded promptly. We give his own words as to his feelings when the great change came. Dr. Johnson was asking him questions while his soul was enveloped in gloom, and almost despair. He says: "He continued to ask until I suppose he saw clearly my state of mind. He then turned my mind to view Christ in his true character, and what he has done as man's security in order to meet and satisfy the law in man's stead. Every word seemed to shed light on the subject. My mind followed him until it was finished. It seemed that a shock of lightning poured through my whole frame, and I thought it was really so (a storm was raging at the time); but I saw the plan of salvation complete, full and free. I saw God could be just and save sinners, for what Christ had done." He seems, however, not to have received the idea that he had really any change at this time. He saw how he *could* be saved, but yet he did not believe he had complied with the terms of the gospel. He continues: "I continued in this state of mind some four weeks or more, when, at a camp-meeting in Union county, Ky., such a sense of divine love, mercy, goodness, and glory of God burst upon my view as to overpower me. I broke forth into expressions of wonder, joy, and gladness. For a time I was so completely lost in the love of the Savior that I knew not what I did." Mr. Knight returned home, immediately erected the family altar, and resolved he would not drink ardent spirits (although at this time there were no temperance organizations in the country).

He soon began to feel that the Lord had something for him to do in his vineyard which he had not done. He felt a burning anxiety for souls. But he was very poor, had a young and increasing family largely dependent on his efforts for their every day support, and it looked like utter folly, he thought, for such an ignorant and poor man as he was to think of any position in the Church but that of a modest private member. We quote again: "My impressions to warn the unconverted and to try to save sinners continually increased; but I had no knowledge of anything as a science. I had a little superficial knowledge of reading, writing, arithmetic, and nothing more. I had no proper knowledge of the nature and form of letters, and the proper method of spelling words, nor of forming words into a sentence scientifically. Here was my ignorance, poverty, and the weight of a rising family entirely dependent upon my energies for management and support in their helpless and dependent condition, and last, but not least, the awful responsibility of the work. These, all combined, presented obstacles which, to my mind, seemed insurmountable in my peculiar circumstances." To add to this formidable array of difficulties, his health had declined and he was in debt. To human vision these were enough to appall the mind of any one. But the promised "sufficient grace" can surmount all obstacles and remove all mountains.

Mr. Knight finally broke the subject to his wife, fearing she would oppose his efforts to preach; but he was much disappointed in her cheerful willingness for him to do any thing he felt to be duty. Accordingly, in the Spring of 1821 he went to Kentucky to attend the meeting of Logan Presbytery. He was received as a candidate, and from that time Providence seemed to smile on his plans for a living for his family. He set about the study of English Grammar (Murray) without a teacher. He worked hard at manual labor all day, and sat up late and studied his Grammar. Then he arose in the morning before light. He rode on horseback two hundred miles that Fall to attend Presbytery. At the next session (which was a year from his reception as a candidate) he was licensed at Rose Creek, Hopkins county, Ky., with eleven others, to preach the gospel as a probationer. He rode the circuit and preached as much as possible, in his straightened circumstances. Ministers in those days got very little sustenance. Indeed the congregations were few, poor, and scattered over a broad territory. When Cumberland Synod ordered the organization of Illinois Presbytery the first Tuesday in May, 1823, Mr. Knight, with others, was transferred to the care of the new Presbytery. He was present at its organization. We have often heard him describe the occasion.

It will be seen, therefore, that Mr. Knight, as a minister, began with the beginning of our Church in Illinois. No man was better acquainted with its toils, difficulties, and discouragements than was he.

The acquaintance of Mr. Knight with the writer dates back to the Spring of 1849. We then met first in the General Assembly. We had corresponded before. We were placed together on a committee to try to adjust the difficulties arising out of the famous "White and Bonham" case. In 1853 we met again near Edwardsville, at old Goshen church, in a meeting; and shortly after the writer became a member of the same Presbytery, and our relations were henceforth necessarily intimate. Mr. Knight lived to a good old age, and departed to his long home on the 2nd of February, 1876, at his residence in Donnellson, Montgomery county, where he had resided for some years. His death was very peaceful and quiet, without a struggle or seeming pain. He was not able to speak after he was taken ill, and died in a few minutes; but his whole life was a "living epistle," to be known and read by all men. He had lost his first wife several years previous, after having reared a large family. She was a good woman, full of faith, and a help-meet indeed. After being single for a good while Mr. Knight was married to Mrs. Eliza Barber, the widow of Rev. John Barber, Jr., who still survives him. She, too, is a most consecrated, pious lady. His last years were spent free from want, temporal and spiritual, and he went down to the grave beloved by the entire Cumberland Presbyterian Church throughout the State, and mourned by many others besides. He lived to see one Presbytery spread into ten, and a "handful of corn" in the top of the mountains shake its fruit like Lebanon. At the Fall session of Vandalia Presbytery of 1876, of which he had been a member from its organization, that body, in memory of his long, respected and useful life, ordered a funeral sermon to be preached by the writer, which was done before a large and tearful assembly of people, after suitable resolutions had been placed upon the record in regard to his death.

We append the following reflections: Mr. Knight in personal appearance was a hearty, stout, robust man, and at the time of his death would probably weigh nearly two hundred pounds. He was rather slow of speech, but always left the impression upon his hearers that he had thought closely on the subject before he spoke. He was not a fluent speaker or an orator, and yet there was something about his appearance which always and everywhere commanded the respect and attention of the people.

He was a man of very positive convictions.  He formed his own opinions regardless of what others might think or not think of the subject in question; and he had the moral courage to do what he thought was right, if he stood alone. He was not strict in parliamentary rules, but he was a good counsellor in the judicatories of the Church, and spent nearly his entire time in studying ways and means to do good.  He was well versed in the Scriptures, and had as clear an idea of the theological position of our Church as any man with whom we ever conversed or read after.  He was a man of unusual power in prayer, and many times in the application of his sermon he was powerful and convincing.  He always used scrupulously good and chaste language, and we never knew him to descend to the low jesting and joking in private circles which so often injure ministerial character and influence.  He was one of the oldest citizens of the country, as he was one of the oldest ministers of any denomination, and he carried with him to the grave a character untainted by a single spot through a long and variously active life.  He always took a deep interest and bore an active part in sustaining every enterprise of the Church; and, while he loved and had the confidence of all Christians who knew him, he was a firm and unflinching Cumberland Presbyterian in principle, and believed that the doctrinal standpoint of our Church was the point towards which all Christendom, in its theological changes, is tending.  In all the relations of life Mr. Knight acquitted himself with like credit.  He was the kind husband, the affectionate father, the friendly neighbor, the good citizen, the Christian gentleman, the faithful, successful minister of Christ.

### REV. SAMUEL M'ADOW.

This name is familiar to all who ever read about Cumberland Presbyterians, he being one of the immortal three who had the courage to face public opinion and the frowns of the "mother Church," and act out his conscious convictions of right, regardless of the applause or censure of the world. At his humble home in Dixon county, Tennessee, Feb. 4th, 1810, the Cumberland Presbytery was re-organized, and another feeble denomination started in its career in the world for good or ill.

As the venerable Dr. Beard, in his second series of Biographical Sketches, has already given the Church and the world a sketch of this father in Israel, this would have been deemed sufficient by the writer, but for the fact that Mr. McAdow spent the last years of his life in Illinois, and his body lies sleeping in Illinois soil. We regard any attempt at a history of the Church in this State as defective and incomplete, without reference to this father also. For the facts of his earlier days herein noted, we are mainly indebted to the sketch by Dr. Beard.

Mr. McAdow was born April 10, 1760, in Guilford county, North Carolina. His father's name was John, and his mother's maiden name was Ellen Nelson. They were of Scotch-Irish descent, and were Presbyterians, members of Buffalo congregation, of which Rev. David Caldwell was pastor. Mr. McAdow's mother died when he was about ten years of age. When about eleven years of age he professed religion and joined Mr. Caldwell's church. He was living on a farm, but when quite young he was placed at Mr. Caldwell's school for a regular and thorough education. The Revolutionary War broke up the school for a time, but after it was over he resumed his studies and completed an academic course. He afterwards attended for three years the Mecklenburg College, where he finished his education. In the meantime his father died. He returned home to the farm, and on Nov. 24th, 1788, was married to Henrietta Wheatley. Five children were the result of this union, all but one dying in infancy.

His impressions to preach the gospel began shortly after he professed religion, but he did not begin the preparation till after he was head of a family. He began the study of theology under Dr. Caldwell, and on the 20th of September, 1794, he was licensed to preach by the Presbytery of Orange, the oldest Presbytery in North Carolina. In this Presbytery at the time of his licensure were Mr. McGready, William McGee, William Hodge, and others, who figured largely in after years in the revival measures and times of the Cumberland country. He was ordained by the same Presbytery, but the exact time is not known. It was prior to 1799. He was for a time pastor of Hopewell. congregation, in North Carolina. His wife died April 20th, 1799. After this sad event he turned his attention to the Western country, several acquaintances and a number of relatives having already gone to Kentucky. He started in 1799, but stopped one Summer in East Tennessee, during which time he preached to a congregation called Big Limestone. This congregation was exceedingly anxious for him to remain their pastor, but his mind was fixed upon Kentucky, and therefore in the Fall he came on to Kentucky, and found the great revival in full blast. He preached to Red River church in Logan county, and Rock Bridge in Christian county.

He was married the second time to a Miss Catherine Clark, of Logan county, a very pious woman. One child, a daughter, was the fruit of this marriage. On the 17th of May, 1804, his second wife died. Committing his two little daughters to the care of a sister, he traveled and preached extensively, and thus continued until he became almost entirely disabled by an affection of the lungs. In July, 1806, he married the third time to Miss Hannah Coke. Two sons resulted from this marriage. He now bought land and settled in Dixon county, Tennessee, and taught school. Here he remained till 1815. He was residing here at the ever memorable period of the organization of the Cumberland Presbyterian Church. To quote the very appropriate language of Dr. Beard, "The house has become historical.

It was an unpretending building on the bank of Jones Creek, about seven miles from Charlotte. The good men who prayed and acted on that occasion had no conception of what the result would be."—Beard's Sketches, page 11.

After the year 1815 he lived a short time in Jackson county. In 1828 he removed to Bond county, Illinois. From age and infirmity he seldom preached here, but never failed to throw his influence at all times in favor of religion. On June 3d, 1839, he lost his third wife.

He became a member of Vandalia Presbytery in rather an irregular way. We do not find anywhere on the records when he joined by letter or otherwise. There may be such record, and we have overlooked it. The action of Presbytery making him a member has been recorded elsewhere. Father McAdow had been in the country about ten years, and was in it when the Presbytery was organized; but there is no mention of his name. Perhaps his age and infirmities prevented him from attending, and the meetings of the Presbytery were seldom near his residence. He was sixty-eight years old when he first settled in Illinois. From the time of the death of his last wife he seemed to fall into a rather gloomy and despondent mood, not about the Church or the cause of Christ, but about his own home enjoyments. Still, he occasionally preached, and his last sermon was from the text, "Follow peace with all men, and holiness, without which no man shall see the Lord." It was published in full in the *Theological Medium* of 1846. His last words are reported to have been, "All is peace. My work is done. Everything is ready. I have nothing to do but to die. There is no doubt, no fear." Suitable resolutions were passed in relation to his death by the Presbytery at its next session, and a funeral discourse was preached to his memory by Rev. John Barber. His grave is in the cemetery at old Mt. Gilead church, in Bond county. Many of his grand-children live in that country yet. It has been our good fortune to look upon that little mound of earth several times, and never without the most strange and thrilling emotions. A neat, respectable tombstone has been placed at the grave by his relatives.

Mr. McAdow seems never to have been a "son of thunder," like Ewing and King, yet, while modest and unusually diffident for one of his opportunities and abilities, he was firm and 'steadfast in his convictions of what was right. He was a man of fair abilities as a preacher, pretty well educated for the times in which he lived, and a man of unspotted character. He lacked only a little of eighty-eight years when he died. Had it not been for his decision, the Cumberland Presbyterian Church might not have existed. Who can read the thrilling statement of his anxious, all-night prayer for light and guidance before the organization, without feeling that he was no ordinary man, and his no ordinary degree of piety. Wherever the "medium theology" shall be known and the Cumberland Presbyterian Church shall be heard of, the name and character of Samuel McAdow will stand out in letters of living light, and, we doubt not, will be handed down to generations yet unborn as one of the great moral heroes of the country and of the Western continent.

### REV. JAMES ASHMORE.

James Ashmore was born in Jefferson county, Tennessee, August 17, 1807. He removed to Illinois at an early day, professed religion in 1831 or 1832 while living on Pigeon Creek, Clark county, and the same Fall united with the church of which Rev. Isaac Hill was pastor. He joined Vandalia Presbytery in June, 1833, at Mount Zion, Macon county, was licensed to preach Oct. 17, 1835, at old Union (now Irving) church in Montgomery county by the same Presbytery, and was ordained by the same Presbytery at Beaver Creek church on the 10th of October, 1837. Rev. Daniel Traughber preached the ordination sermon from Mal. ii. 7, and Rev. Joel Knight presided and gave the charge.

When Foster Presbytery was organized Mr. Ashmore became a member, and continues to be a member. His home is in Fairmount, Vermillion county.

Few men in the church, for his opportunities, have been as useful. When he began operations in that country forty years since, it was a wilderness, spiritually and naturally. Mr. Ashmore has been a great revivalist. He organized the first Cumberland Presbyterian church in that country, from which a large number of other congregations has sprung. Thousands have been converted under his ministrations, and he is still laboring with zeal and success, although he is more than three score and ten years old.

In a conversation with the writer he said his father was raised up in the Catholic faith, and when he was a boy a Catholic priest visited the family, and urged the parents to let him have James, and he would take him to Rome and educate him for the priesthood. The father consented, but, when the time drew near to start for Italy, Mrs. Ashmore protested so strongly against giving up her boy that the project was finally relinquished by the priest, but evidently with reluctance. He also stated that he was under the power of conviction for sin for five years before relief came to his mind. He had a great desire and a wonderful temptation to make money and let the ministry go, and only gave it up after he had lost all his property. Another remarkable incident in his history was the conversion of his father under his preaching. The old gentleman became so interested about his soul that he followed up his son's appointments on the circuit, and embraced the Saviour at one of them.

Mr. Ashmore has been married three times. He was first married to Miss Catherine Armstrong May 15, 1828, at her father's residence. His second wife was Sarah M. Newman, Oakland, Illinois, and his present wife was Rebecca I. Grimes. All of his wives were natives of the State of Tennessee. He has eight living children by the first wife, one by the second, and five by the last—fourteen in all. Several are dead.

Mr. Ashmore rode the circuit four years, and settled in Vermillion county in 1842. He organized Mount Pisgah church, the oldest one of Cumberland Presbyterians in the county, to which he preached twenty-nine years as pastor or supply without any interval; and at another time three years more, making *thirty-two* in all that he was the faithful shepherd of this flock. It is questionable whether there is to be found another connection between pastor and people in the State of equal length.

Mr. Ashmore has been a man of excellent constitution. For the most part he has enjoyed good health, and has done an immense amount of ministerial labor without being remunerated for his services as he deserved. He has organized thirty congregations, and about four thousand five hundred souls have professed faith in Christ under the influence of his ministrations. One of his sons, Rev. H. H. Ashmore, is also an esteemed and very useful minister of the gospel.

Father Ashmore never claimed to be an orator or a man of learning, his opportunities for an education being very limited. But he is claimed by others, and justly, too, as one of the most earnest, industrious, and successful ministers in the State. Though the prime of his life was spent in building up the Church in a new and sparsely settled country, and he received from the Church only a pittance in the way of support, yet God blessed his worldly plans so that he and his family had plenty; and it is believed that he is in comfortable circumstances at this writing. With the exception of his hearing, which is somewhat impaired, he retains his usual health and vigor, although in his seventy-first year. We should have mentioned that at his ordination Rev. Samuel McAdow, one of the original three founders of the denomination, was present and participated in the services.

## REV. WILLIAM FINLEY.

Rev. William Finley was born in Warren county, Ky., on the 30th of November, 1800. His parents were pious people and members of the Presbyterian Church. His mother died when he was an infant, and for a few years he was nursed and brought up by Mary Taylor, an aunt. His father in a few years married again, and removed to Robertson county, Tennessee. The reader will remember that these were the times of the great revival of 1800, which originated in this country and swept all over it. Mr. Finley when quite young was the subject of deep and abiding convictions, but seems not to have experienced a change of heart until he was a grown man and married. It is proper to state here that the father of Mr. Finley early became a member of the Cumberland Presbyterian Church, and of course was a decided advocate of the revival measures of that day.

While quite young—but at what period we are not informed—he was united in marriage to Miss Elizabeth Hutchings, and soon thereafter removed to Illinois and settled in Bond county. His wife and several brothers and sisters had become deeply pious, and felt and manifested great interest for his salvation. Since a child he had been the constant subject of deep conviction for sin, and often had great wrestlings of soul on the subject. Not until the month of October, 1825, did he make up his mind fully to seek God and cast all his care upon him. It was at old Bethel church, in Bond county, at a sacramental meeting held by Presbyterians, and in which Cumberland Presbyterians also united and labored earnestly, that Mr. Finley found the "pearl of great price." An old memorandum, furnished us by his son, Dr. W. M. Finley, of Salem, Ill., tells us that on Sabbath night of that meeting, Oct. 6, 1825, he made a full surrender of all to Christ, after having a very clear and impressive sense of his lost and utterly helpless condition. For some days after he experienced this great change he was not fully satisfied, fearing he had been deceived and the change was not what God in his Word required. He therefore prayfully read the Bible, and with great searchings of heart wrestled with God for a positive assurance of his safety and peace with God. This blessed assurance finally came so plain and satisfactory that he could no longer doubt. Happy would it be for the Christian Church now, if all young converts would thus carefully examine the foundation of their hopes. To use his own words: "This great question being satisfactorily settled, I at once took up my cross, and engaged with trembling anxiety in the discharge of Christian duty." He first erected the family altar, and there offered his morning and evening sacrifice to God for himself and family. He next engaged in active work in whatever way he could do good in the revival which was going on in the neighborhood. In conversation, prayer and exhortation he was very active and very useful. Mr. Finley records that for some years after his conversion he was sometimes the subject of deep gloom and perplexing doubts about the genuineness of his change. But searching the Scriptures and fervent prayer enabled him finally to dispel these seasons of gloom, and entertain an unshaken confidence and assurance that he was "accepted in the Beloved."

Not long after his conversion and union with the Church he felt impressions to preach the gospel. About this time Mr. Finley's mind was greatly agitated with the doctrinal questions so rife in that period. On the one hand, the old system of decrees and election, as taught in the Westminster standards, (which, after a thorough investigation, he decided to mean nothing less than absolute fatality,) he found he must reject if he believed the plain teachings of God's Word. On the other hand, the apostasy plank in the Arminian system seemed to his mind a great discouragement to a penitent sinner. Being greatly perplexed with these doctrines on either hand, he says in his memoranda, "My mind found a suitable remedy as exhibited in what is sometimes termed the middle-ground system, rejecting the extremes of both the Calvinistic and Arminian systems." He kept on examining and sifting these doctrines until he became thoroughly convinced of the truth of the doctrinal stand-point of Cumberland Presbyterians, which position he preached with great zeal, fervor and success for many years afterward. His choosing his Church was wholly from principle, and not merely social circumstances or human policy.

The following letter from his son, W. M. Finley, M. D., of Salem, Ill., is in no respect an exaggeration of the industry and success of this laborious servant of God. It is due to the truth of history, however, to record, that in the latter part of Mr. Finley's life, on account of trouble which arose in his Presbytery, he withdrew from the Cumberland Presbyterian Church, and was not re-united with it. But all who were conversant with his preaching and his feelings testify that he carried with him to the grave his early attachment to the Cumberland Presbyterian Church and her doctrines. It was an unfortunate occurrence which severed his connection with us, but of the right or the wrong of his course in this matter we desire to spend no opinion. He was not what the world would call a learned or eloquent preacher, but he was what was perhaps better: a truly spiritual, devoted minister of Jesus—one than whom few men have been more successful in winning souls to Christ. To say that he had his weak places and made blunders, is but to acknowledge what is applicable to the best of men. Of Mr. Finley's family we know but little, save that he was married twice. His last companion yet survives. Of the children by the first wife we have no knowledge, except of the very worthy son who furnished the interesting letter mentioned below, and to whom we are indebted for nearly all the information obtained respecting the life of his father.

"Rev. Wm. Finley, after he made a profession of religion

October 25, 1825, united with the Cumberland Presbyterian Church, and was soon after received under the care of Illinois Presbytery as a probationer to preach the gospel. How long he was a probationer and when he was licensed to preach I know not.* But I have often heard him relate the trials and hardships under which he labored to support his family, and acquire a sufficient knowledge of the various branches of study required by the Book of Discipline in order to fit him for ordination.

"My earliest recollection of my father is, that he was seldom at home. His stay at home was always more like a visit than anything else. He never took much interest in or trouble about the cares pertaining to the small farm on which he resided. My mother always superintended the farm work. If mother had not been one of the most industrious of women, and an extra good manager of farming and finance, father could never have given all his time and talents to the interests of the Church. His compensation was so small that the wants of the family would have compelled him to seek some other means for their support. At this period (about 1840) father traveled and preached all the time. His preaching tours generally extended from six weeks to two months, during which time he was never at home. He was then living in Pleasant Prairie, Bond county, where he resided about ten years. In 1843 he removed to VanBurensburgh, on the old stage road from Vandalia to Hillsboro. Here he taught school during the Winter of 1843-4, and preached every Saturday and Sabbath, and often one or more evenings during the week, in the village and the adjacent neighborhood.

---

*For the date of his reception and licensure see the minutes of Illinois Presbytery, published in the first part of this work. He was ordained with Rev. Isaac Hill by Vandalia Presbytery at Mt. Zion June 18, 1833. Rev. Joel Knight preached the ordination sermon, Rev. John Barber, Jr., presided, and Rev. John Barber, Sr., gave the charge. We quote from the records.— EDITOR.

"In the Spring of 1844 he went to Salem, Ill. He had been visiting said place for several years, and preaching in various parts of Marion county. In 1840 I think he organized a congregation called Mt. Carmel (now Kinmundy), the first Cumberland Presbyterian organization ever made in said county. After locating in Salem he soon organized a congregation called Bethel, seven miles east of Salem, and in 1846 he organized a congregation in Salem, and, through his own labor and exertion, the congregation erected the first house of worship ever put up in Salem. All that the Salem congregation ever was, or now is, is mainly due to his untiring efforts in its behalf. He continued to preach in Marion county and the adjoining counties for about twenty years, and by him and his unceasing efforts McLin Presbytery was organized, to supply the field of labor that he had mainly been instrumental in opening up to Cumberland Presbyterianism. He organized congregations in Fayette, Clay, Jefferson, Wayne, White and Edwards counties during his ministry, which formed the principal field of his labors, and most of which is included in the bounds of McLin Presbytery. He was untiring in his work, going from house to house and place to place, preaching daily. I think that the statement is strictly true, that for thirty years of his ministry he averaged as much as one sermon per day. He once showed me his memorandum book, kept for five years just preceding his locating in Salem. He had preached on an average one and a half times each day for the five years, traveled twelve miles each day, and had received as remuneration $143 per year. I have often thought that he could visit more families, shake more people by the hand in one day, than any modern politican can on the eve of an important election. Such was his daily life for over forty long, weary years. He devoted all his time and energies both of body and mind, to the cause of the blessed Redeemer. In his early ministry his voice was strong and his zeal unbounded, and as such he was a successful revivalist. Camp and protracted meetings were never complete in his field of operations, unless 'Uncle Billy Finley,' as he was familiarly called, was there to do much of the preaching.

"One distinguishing feature in his life was the great influence he had over wicked men. They all respected and loved him. Many of them would loan him money on his own note, or often on his own word. They would defend him on all occasions when necessary, and contribute liberally to his support, even when unsolicited by any one. Though father was always poor financially, and often borrowed money in small sums, he always had good credit, and always paid his debts promptly and according to contract.

"He continued his ministerial labors until his death. He never, from my earliest recollection, engaged in any business to make money, and seemed not to regard money in any other light than a means to supply pressing wants, get books, and enable him to preach the gospel. He taught school only a few quarter sessions, and that was only to enable him to supply the direst wants of his family, or get the much-coveted books.

"The last sermon he ever preached was in the Presbyterian church in Salem, a few days before his death. He was on a visit to his children in Salem, having some three years before located in Williamson county, Ill. He died on the 23d day of November, 1870, being seventy years old lacking but seven days. His last sickness was of short duration. Just before his death it is said by those present that he seemed to be gone for several moments, and then to revive for a short time, and clearly and plainly describe, in glowing terms, the appearance of Moses, Daniel and St. Paul—his three favorite Bible characters. He also told of hearing the sweet music of heaven; and then, after such living testimony to the truth of the religion he had so long preached, he passed away with a sweet smile on his face. And thus my father died, in full hope of endless happiness. I was not permitted to be present with him in his last hours, but from the testimony of those present I can but feel that he died a happy and triumphant death, and entered into that rest prepared for the redeemed in heaven."

# CHAPTER XIV.

### BIOGRAPHICAL.

From the pen of Rev. W. D. Dodds, of Chilicothe, Mo., we have the following interesting sketch of his father,

### REV. GILBERT DODDS.

"Rev. Gilbert Dodds was born in Spartinburg District, South Carolina, on the 6th day of June, 1793. He was the seventh son of Francis Dodds. His father's family started on their journey from Carolina to Western Kentucky, but the father sickened and died on the route, and was buried at the foot of Spencer's Hill, a spur of Cumberland mountains. The widow and family continued their journey, and arrived, without any other misfortune, in the land of their destination. Here, in this then sparsely settled and comparatively wild region, the subject of this sketch was reared to manhood.

"In a new country, where the principal attention is given to the erection of dwellings and opening farms, the education of the youth, to a great extent, is lost sight of. Hence, the subject of our sketch enjoyed but few advantages for acquiring an education. But being of an aspiring mind, and passionately fond of reading, he left no stone unturned in the pursuit of knowledge. With the aid of a Winter term at the common school of his neighborhood, he obtained a knowledge of the primary branches of an English education.

"About the time he arrived at the years of manhood, in his eager search for reading matter he fell in with Tom Paine's 'Age of Reason' and Volney's 'Ruins.' The perusal of these infidel works, as he often remarked, came very near ruining his soul. But, in the wise Providence of God, whose inscrutable wisdom had marked him out as one of his chosen vessels, he was thrown under the powerful ministry of the Rev. Finis Ewing. This faithful embassador of Christ, who knew all the lurking-places of the infidel, by his logical reasoning and powerful gospel appeals, soon scattered the sophistries of Paine, Volney, and all the hosts of the opposers of our holy religion, to the four winds. The faithful preaching of this man of God led to deep and serious thought, and, after a series of severe mental struggles, he finally yielded himself into the hands of a merciful Redeemer. Not long after he embraced religion he, to the best of my knowledge, united with the old Bethlehem congregation of the Cumberland Presbyterian Church.

"In his 22d year he was united in marriage with Miss Mary Clinton, of Crittenden county, Ky. Their union was in all respects a happy one. They walked the pathway of life together almost fifty-one years, and raised a family of seven sons and five daughters, all of whom they lived to see grow up to manhood and womanhood. The wife and mother departed this life in her sixty-sixth year in the triumph of a living faith in Christ, having been a member of the Cumberland Presbyterian Church over forty-three years.

"At what date the subject of our sketch united with Presbytery and commenced the preparation for the ministry we are not able to say. The name of the Presbytery, however, we are pretty sure was old Logan, the Presbytery in which old father William Harris lived, labored and died. In the year 1824 he removed from Kentucky to Sangamon county, Illinois. Here he united with Revs. John M. Berry and Thomas Campbell in organizing Sangamon Presbytery.* During the early years of his ministry in Illinois he labored extensively in camp-meetings, and assisted in planting a great many congregations in Central Illinois. He often conducted camp-meetings without any ministerial assistance. We have often heard him say he had to travel one hundred miles to camp-meetings and Presbytery. After camp-meetings came into disuse he labored extensively in protracted meetings. His labors in protracted meetings were confined mostly to the counties of Menard and Sangamon. He was always a zealous advocate of temperance, and in the later years of his life he delivered many lectures on the subject, and aided extensively in organizing temperance societies.

"The last eight or nine years of his life his health became so feeble that his Presbytery (Sangamon) passed an order that he attend its sessions at discretion; but he always made it a point, although in feeble health, to attend Presbytery, and take part in its deliberations. During the last five years of his life he was threatened with paralysis, which finally terminated his life on the third day of May, 1872, he wanting only one month and three days of being seventy-nine years of age. During the last years of his life he seemed to enjoy much of the comforts of that blessed religion which he had preached to others in the prime of life, and in his last hours gave strong evidence of its power to conquer the last enemy, and administer an abundant entrance into the everlasting kingdom of our Lord and Savior, Jesus Christ."

### REV. DAVID FOSTER.

The subject of this sketch was born in Rowan county, North Carolina, May 4th, 1780. His parents were William and Nancy Foster. They were poor, but pious, and early

---

*Mr. Dodds was placed under the care of Illinois Presbytery at its organization as a candidate. For date of ordination see minutes of said Presbytery published elsewhere.—EDITOR.

instructed their son in the principles of Christianity. When quite young David became a member of a Presbyterian church, of which Rev. Dr. McCorkle was pastor. In 1797 the family removed to Sumner county, Tennessee, and settled in the neighborhood of old Shiloh church, to which they presented their letters. Rev. William McGee was pastor. They were all—parents and son—examined as to their experimental religion, in addition to their letters. The parents were received, but the son advised to re-examine the foundation of his hope. This he did, with the conclusion that he was not a Christian. He began to seek Christ as never before, and at home, in a quiet way, found peace with God, and soon became prominent in his efforts to win souls to Jesus.

He became a candidate under old Cumberland Presbytery, and at old Red River meeting house was licensed to preach the gospel October 2d, 1805. Some time before his licensure he had traveled as a licensed "exhorter," in supplying the great destitutions of that day. Of course he, among others, fell under the ban of the famous "commission" of Kentucky Synod; yet he continued his labors under the "council" which succeeded the dissolution of the Presbytery, and never did he seem to labor with more success than in those dark days.

In the Summer of 1806 he was married to Miss Ann Beard, of Sumner county, who was a noble Christian woman, full of faith, devoutly consecrated to the Master, and a good help-meet for her husband. In 1808 Mr. Foster moved to Wilson county, and settled in Suggs Creek congregation. Shortly after the re-organization of Cumberland Presbytery he was set apart to the whole work of the ministry July 27, 1810, at the Suggs Creek church, and at the same time was installed pastor of that church. He also preached to two other churches a part of the time during his pastorate, until 1824. A large portion of his time was spent annually in attending camp and protracted meetings, to which he was appointed by his Presbytery.

In 1827 he removed to Illinois, where it was little else than a vast wilderness. Dr. Beard says, (Biographical Sketches, vol. 1, page 66,) that both he and his wife were anti-slavery in their feelings and views, and gives this as one reason for his removal to Illinois. He first settled in Sangamon county, afterwards in Macon county, and for a time was colporteur for the American Tract Society. He was on a visit to St. Louis May 7th, 1833, the year cholera first visited that city, to get a fresh supply of books. On his way home the next day he was attacked with cholera and died on Silver Creek, Madison county, the 9th of May, 1833. He was buried near by where he died. He was away from home, but he had friends with him who did all in their power to save him. He retained his consciousness to the last, and died resigned and peaceful. His death was a heavy stroke to the few and scattered churches in this country. No man was more beloved by the people than he.

Mr. Foster has left his mark all over the churches of Illinois. He was first a member of Illinois Presbytery, where his seat was never vacant unless he was hindered by Providence. When Sangamon Presbytery was organized he became a member of that Presbytery; and when Vandalia was organized he fell within her bounds. He organized the churches at Mt. Zion and Bethany, from which many large and prosperous congregations have gone forth. Many others were fostered by him. It may well be said that his praise was in all the churches. Many are found now who revere his memory. It was never the privilege of the writer to meet with him; but, what is perhaps better, he has met with his works all over the country. "He, being dead, yet speaketh." Evidently he was a devoted man. He lived every day for the Lord and his cause. Though not a brilliant preacher, yet he was a preacher of more than ordinary intelligence, zeal and success. As a worthy testimonial to his memory, Central Illinois Synod—Vandalia Presbytery in particular—have provided the means to have the old decaying limestone rocks, which were at first placed at his grave, supplanted by respectable modern marble tombstones. It is not known to the writer whether his companion or any of his six children are living; nor, if living, where they reside.

The action of Vandalia Presbytery in regard to his death may be found elsewhere. At the session of Illinois Synod which met at Pisgah meeting house, St. Louis county, Mo., October 17, 1833, we find the following appropriate record of Mr. Foster's death:

"WHEREAS, it has pleased the great Head of the Church to remove by death from the councils and labors of this Synod the Rev. David Foster, the Moderator of the former session, and one of her most aged and useful members;

*Resolved*, therefore, that this Synod feel deeply sensible of the bereavement occasioned by this solemn dispensation of divine Providence, and that the Synod cherish with very fond remembrance the memory of her dear departed fellow-laborer." The minute in both instances is short, but is a true expression of what was felt in reference to this good man. The men of those days were men of comparatively few words, but they said nothing they did not mean.

### REV. WOODS M'COWAN HAMILTON.

His son gives the following:

"Some time in the year 1790 my grand-parents started to move from Virginia to Kentucky, but, in consequence of troubles with the Cherokee Indians, they stopped on Little Pigeon, in Severe county, East Tennessee, where my father, Woods McCowan Hamilton, was born, on the 3d day of June, 1791. He was the youngest of eight sons and one daughter, there being one daughter younger than he. Grandfather died in 1799; and as that part of Kentucky (Livingstone county) was sparsely settled, my father had but little chance of attending school. I think about six months' irregular schooling is about all he ever had.

"After grand-mother died, my father, a lad of perhaps thirteen or fourteen, came to Illinois to live with an older brother, Patrick Hamilton, who was engaged in making salt on the Saline in Gallatin county. While thus engaged he was sent by his brother, in company with another man, on foot back to his old home in Kentucky. It was in the Winter. The waters had been very high and had frozen over. Then it snowed, so that the road could not be seen. They got lost, and were without fire or food for over two days; and when at last they got to a house my father's feet were frozen so badly that it was over six months before he could stand on them, having lost nearly half his toes, which rendered him a cripple through life. During this affliction he obtained books, and made considerable progress in the elementary branches. So strong was his thirst for knowledge, that after he got able to work he spent every night in study by the light of a burning pine knot. In a few years he commenced teaching, which afforded him better opportunities of study and improvement.

"During these years, and while, as he says, he was very wicked, he became acquainted with my mother, Jane M. McCluskey. Through her influence he became deeply convicted, and after a hard struggle of over six weeks was converted, and joined the Presbyterian Church. Afterward in 1811 he and my mother were married. On the 29th of November, 1812, I was born, and was baptized by the Rev. David Dickey, a Presbyterian minister. In about 1818 father, having for a long time been deeply impressed that it was his duty to preach, and, although a pretty thorough English scholar, having no hope of ever being qualified in accordance with the standard of the old Church, withdrew his connection and joined the Cumberland Presbyterians. Soon he was admitted as a candidate in Logan Presbytery, and was sent as a missionary to Illinois. I think he must have spent two or three years in this work before he moved his family, which he did in the Spring of 1822. The first Summer the family lived in Thom's Prairie, on Enoch Beach's Farm, in Wayne county. The next Fall we moved to Long Prairie, same county, lived through the Winter and next Summer, and in that Fall moved to Burnt Prairie, in White county, where we lived for over twenty-five years, and where my mother died in 1832. In 1845 or 1846 the family started to move to Jonesboro, Union county, but on account of sickness had to stop over for one year in Williamson county. My father died at his farm two miles north of Jonesboro station, on the Illinois Central railroad, on February 7th, 1865, and was buried at Jonesboro.

"During his first year as missionary to Illinois I think he was associated with another minister, but I do not know who. Afterward W. H. McCluskey, a cousin of my mother, and James S. Alexander were each sent out with him. Afterward McCluskey went to Indiana, where he labored successfully for many years. In early Spring of 1822, just before we left Kentucky, my father was ordained by Logan Presbytery. Of his missionary labors I can say but little, as I was too young to understand much; but from what I have since learned I think he was very successful. In fact, I have met with quite a number who became acquainted with him in those days, and they all seemed to think and speak of him in the highest terms.

"After we moved to Illinois I do not recollect that he spent much of his time in missionary work—at least, not after the first three or four years—but was always engaged in preaching some place on Sunday, and very often the Saturday previous. In thinking back, although it is a good many years, I cannot now remember of my father being idle on the Sabbath, unless he or some of the family was sick, or there was a meeting in our church at which other ministers were present. In fact, I think I may safely say that during his long life he spent it all in preaching and laboring to save men from sin and death. He was always poor, and had to engage in any pursuit which promised a support for his large family. I recollect during my early years that he made all the shoes for his family. Afterward he obtained a set of tools and worked at the carpenter business during the Fall and Winter. We always lived on a farm, and during the Summer were engaged in farming operations as long as I remained at home, and, in fact, until they moved to Jonesboro.

"In those days people never thought of, or at least did not give the preacher anything for his services, particularly money. Sometimes a sister would give a pair of socks, the cloth for a vest, a pair of pants, or some other article, which were always very acceptable. I recollect that once a man in Seven Mile Prairie, a Mr. Anderson, I think, made and gave my father a pair of calf boots, which lasted him several years for Sunday wear.

"I recollect while living at home of seeing and reading quite a number of poems, songs, and other pieces of his composition, only a few of which can now be found. I also remember that I used to think they were very good, and tried to have him get them printed; but on account of his extreme diffidence he would never consent to do so. Later, he wrote out and had printed a full set of questions and answers on the several branches of examination of licentiates preparatory to ordination, some of which I had, but cannot now find. Several other productions of his I have seen from time to time, but none of them can now be found, except the short sketch of his early life already referred to. My brother tells me that in or about 1856 Bro. Logan, then of Alton, published, bound, and shipped a box of hymn books compiled and composed by my father.* With the two exceptions, I do not know of my father ever having any of his writings published. He seemed to think or feel that they were not worth preserving or (what is likely the true reason) shrank from publicity. In the short sketch already referred to is found this quotation from Pope:

> "'Thus let me live, unseen, unknown;
> Thus unlamented let me die—
> Steal from the world, and not a stone
> To tell where I lie.'"

The writer had a slight acquaintance with Mr. Hamilton before his death, and had been in his company at the judicatories of the Church several times. He was a man of sterling worth. He had more than ordinary diffidence in his deportment in society. Some of his letters on divinity were published in the *Missouri Cumberland Presbyterian*, which always denoted more than usual profundity of thought and clearness of statement in his propositions. He was in the General Assembly in 1863 when the war was raging in all its fury, and when the whole country was intensely agitated over the war questions. The Assembly met in Alton, in the church of which the writer was pastor. The questions of slavery and the rebellion were introduced by a memorial from Ohio Synod. A committee was appointed to consider the memorial, consisting of one from each Synod represented there. They made a report, which was adopted with but two dissenting votes. A motion was then made that the Assembly join in prayer, and that the oldest man present lead the devotions. This was done, and Mr. Hamilton led the prayer, which was eloquent, solemn and exceedingly earnest, and seemed to reach the very throne of the Deity. This was the last time we ever met, or that he ever attended the General Assembly. We know that he was greatly es-

---

*This is a mistake. The writer while in St. Louis published for the author the questions and answers referred to, but not the latter book.—EDITOR.

teemed by his neighbors, irrespective of creed or religious opinions. If there was any one mark which distinguished Mr. Hamilton more than another, it was his humility, his self-abasement. He had an exceedingly low opinion of his own efforts. We greatly regret that we have been able to obtain no more satisfactory account of the life and labors of this dear old father in Israel.

### REV. DANIEL TRAUGHBER.

The following sketch of Mr. Traughber is from the pen of his son-in-law, Mr. R. K. Lansden, of Fredonia, Kansas:

"The subject of this sketch was born in Logan county, Kentucky, May 18, 1800, and professed religion in July, 1821. He was licensed to preach as a minister of the gospel in the Cumberland Presbyterian Church in October, 1824; and four years thereafter (1828) he was ordained and set apart to the whole office of the Christian ministry in the Church until the close of his life. From the time he was licensed to preach until 1836 he officiated in his native State as an efficient minister, when he moved and settled in Macon county, Illinois. Here he took charge of Mt. Zion church, over which he presided for twenty-five years, when he was compelled to resign on account of ill health. For several years after resigning as pastor of Mt. Zion church he was not engaged in the direct and particular work of the ministry, though he preached much, and was very useful in building up the Church in numbers and spiritual strength. In this way he labored until 1872, when he came to Kansas, where he was active and untiring in his ministerial duties until he passed away.

"He was married three times. All three of his companions were excellent Christian women, and all preceded him to the glory land.

"On the evening of the 13th December he and the writer went some five miles from town to hold a temperance meeting in the interest of the Murphy movement. He spoke about an hour with great earnestness. We had a very enthusiastic time and he was very much elated. He had to go one mile to stay all night, and I suppose took cold, which caused a severe attack of an old disease. The children were sent for about seven o'clock. We called three of the best physicians we could get, but all their efforts were of no avail. After I had been in the room a few minutes he called me to him and said: 'Robert, my poor old frame can't stand this long. I want you to call the friends around, and sing and pray, that I may see my way clear; and if God says go, I say go, too.' This was the last he said about his own case. He lingered in great pain until two o'clock on Sabbath morning, when he became unconscious, and continued so until half-past one in the evening, when his spirit took its flight to that upper and better world. He has gone to join his co-laborers—Lansden, Aston, Knight, Bryan, and many others who have gone before. He is missed in this country, where he was very useful. He leaves six children, all of whom are professors of religion except one, and many sorrowing friends; but we mourn not as those having no hope."

The writer will add a few reflections of his own in regard to the deceased. He first became acquainted with Mr. Traughber on the way to the General Assembly, which met in Princeton, Kentucky, in 1853. He and many other delegates were on the same packet which left the warf at St. Louis a few days before the meeting of that body. After arriving at Princeton we were assigned to the same boarding place; and from that on to the end of his life we knew "Uncle Daniel," as he was familiarly called, and knew him well. Few men of our Illinois ministry have done more to build up the Church than Mr. Traughber. He was a genial, warm-hearted, sunny-spirited man. He was a good speaker, always won the respect and attention of his audience, and, like most of his compeers, lived and died with a character untarnished in every particular. He was very successful in getting sinners to act, even when others failed. He was of medium stature, heavily built, and had just enough of the brogue of the foreigner to make his language attractive when speaking. He was a man of unusual energy of character, and while he did a vast amount of preaching he also cultivated and carried on a large farm, in the management of which he seemed always to prosper. He was always prompt and punctual in attendance upon the judicatories of the Church. He was elected Moderator of the first session of Central Illinois Synod, the sessions of which he always attended until he removed beyond her bounds. He died at the residence of Mr. Green Beasley near Fredonia, Kansas, on December 16th, 1877, of affection of the kidneys, at the advanced age of seventy-seven years and seven months. He leaves thousands over all the West to mourn his departure.

### REV. JOHN CRAWFORD.

Father Crawford is now one of the oldest living ministers in the State. He says, "I was born in South Carolina Jan. 31, 1804." The fore part of his letter relating to his father's removal to Kentucky, and the first Cumberland Presbyterian family ever on Illinois soil, will be found in the first part of the volume. He dates his conviction for sin to a sermon Rev. Thomas Campbell preached near Golconda on his way to the Sangamon country in the early part of 1822; professed religion at old Sugar Creek camp-ground the same Fall. We now quote from his manuscript *verbatim:*

"On the 2d day of March, 1825, I united in marriage with Nancy R. Tagert, and moved to Village church, White county, in the bounds of what is now Ewing Presbytery, in September of the same year. In March, 1826, I joined Illinois Presbytery as a candidate, which then embraced the entire State. My progress was slow, being very deficient in literature and means to acquire it. I was licensed at Bear

Creek church, Bond county, September 1831, and settled in Gallatin county the same month. I was ordained at Union Ridge church in March, 1834. My time has been mostly spent in efforts to supply destitute points. I have traveled over some fifteen counties in Southern Illinois, officiated in the organization of seven congregations. My attendance at Church courts has been: General Assemblies, seven; Synodical meetings, sixteen; Presbyteries, one hundred and two; and camp-meetings, one hundred and twenty-eight. I am now in my seventy-fourth year, and have retired, being prostrated by paralysis.

"The following transpired in the bounds of what is now Ewing Presbytery: A camp-meeting was held in the vicinity of Shawneetown at an early date (which I have not) by John Barnett, David Lowry, and others. There were many conversions and a congregation was organized, which was vacated by the removal of General Street, John W. McCord and H. Delaney. Of the remaining members and others the Rev. D. W. McLin organized New Pleasant church in September, 1830, at the present site of New Market. Elders, James Dillard, John Murphy and John V. Sherwood. From this church were stricken off Liberty, Concord, and Walnut Grove, all of which have much declined in the absence of a supply, while the old stand is enfeebled by the change of population."

### REV. J. R. LOWRANCE.

We copy the following brief sketch of this good brother mainly in his own language:

"Jacob Lowrance was my grand-father. His ancestors were Dissenters, and fled from persecution from England to Scotland, thence to Holland, from there to the United States, and settled in the Carolinas. Samuel Lowrance was my father. He was born in South Carolina April 10th, 1792, immigrated to Georgia in early life with his parents, and then to Tennessee, and with his father settled on Bear Creek,

Maury county. There he spent his youthful days. Grandfather and father were elders for years in the Cumberland Presbyterian Church. My father was a convert of the great revival of 1800. He sleeps in Jerseyville cemetery, Jersey county, Illinois.

"Rachel Ramsey, my mother, was born near Nashville, Tennessee, 1781, when it was a small French village, and it was said she was the first white child born there. She was a niece of Col. Rev. Joseph Brown and Joseph Porter, who was a brother of James B. Porter. My mother was also a subject of the revival of 1800, and a member of Rev. Craighead's congregation, but went with the revival party and united with the first Cumberland Presbyterians. She sleeps near Manchester, Morgan county, Illinois.

"I was born in Maury county, Tennessee, April 14, 1818; was baptized by Rev. Robert Donnell (author of 'Donnell's Thought's'). My first serious impressions were received under my father's prayers when he led his four boys with him to secret devotion, I being only seven years of age. They were renewed at old Bear Creek camp-ground, under the shouting and exhortation of my grand-father on Tuesday morning as the meeting was closing when I was ten years old. In the Fall of 1830 I with my parents immigrated to Calaway county, Mo., and there, in old Providence congregation, I was again awakened in Sabbath-school under James Nevins, an elder in said church and my Sabbath-school teacher. On September 2, 1833, at night, I was born into the kingdom of Christ during a camp-meeting held at said church by Eli Guthrie and David Kirkpatrick. O, the bliss and glory of that hour! There my eternal life began, and for over forty years my Savior has led me and kept me, and he will keep me to the end.

"I was then fifteen years, four months and seventeen days old. In the Spring of 1835 I with my parents immigrated to Illinois, and settled near Manchester in Morgan county.

Here on a farm I labored for my father. I was received as a candidate for the ministry by Sangamon Presbytery at Sugar Creek, Sangamon county, April 5, 1837, and wrote three discourses: first from Isaiah lv. 6, then from Romans v. 1, and lastly from Hebrews iv. 9. The Presbytery was composed of J. M. Berry, Thomas Campbell, Gilbert Dodds, Benjamin Canby and A. W. Lansden—five of the noblest men that ever lived. I was licensed at old Concord near Petersburg on September 23, 1838, at a camp-meeting. Benjamin Canby was Moderator. Then for four years and six months I traveled on a circuit extending from Petersburg on the north to Jerseyville on the south. In this time Rev. J. G. White was licensed and came to me, and for years we labored together. I was ordained in company with Bro. J. G. White on the first day of April, 1843, at Sugar Creek, Sangamon county, Illinois. Father Berry delivered the sermon from I. Timothy, iv. 16. From the Fall of 1843 to 1844 I traveled as Synodical missionary and held revival meetings. In the Fall of 1845 I took charge of Stouts Grove and Shiloh congregations, in Mackinaw Presbytery, as supply until the Fall of 1846, on a salary of $160. Then, on the second day of January, 1847, I was, by order of Mackinaw Presbytery, installed pastor of Stouts Grove congregation. Bros. Neill and Archibald Johnson officiated. My salary being $200 and board, many happy days I spent in this congregation. At the General Assembly in 1849 I received the appointment as agent to collect funds for the Home and Foreign Missionary Board. In this work I traveled in Missouri and Illinois. In the Summer of 1850 I preached for Stouts Grove (now Danvers) congregation, and was married November 3d, 1850, to Miss Eliza J. McClure, a member of my charge and daughter of Samuel and Malinda McClure. She was a convert of my first meeting there, and was received into the congregation and baptized by myself. In 1851 I lived and labored in Bloomington, Ill., and but for the want of support there might be to-day a Cumberland Presbyterian church there. In 1853 I removed to Hardin county, Iowa, then on the frontier. In 1857, under the order of Iowa Synod, I located in Oskaloosa. Here I toiled until the Fall of 1866, when I left for Illinois. I stopped a short time at Virginia; then, in April 1867, I located in Lincoln and took charge of Union congregation all my time on a salary of $600. By a request of ministers I left Union congregation and took charge of Danvers congregation Dec. 1, 1867. Here I labored until the Fall of 1870, when I resigned and took charge of Albion congregation, in Edwards county, Illinois. Each of these last congregations gave me $1,000 salary. In Albion I labored until August, 1874, when I returned to Lincoln to school my sons, and took charge of Union and Hopedale (old Shiloh) congregations, where I am now serving the Church as best I can, being sixty years of age in April 14, 1878. Here I am on my way home. Soon my work will be over here below. Rest is near before me."

We will add, that we have known Bro. Lowrance since the Spring of 1849; visited his family not long since and enjoyed their hospitalities. He is still in good health, and bids fair for many years' good service for the Master yet. He is a good preacher, sound in the faith, well received, and never was doing more good than at present.

### REV. CYRUS HAYNES.

The subject of this sketch was born in Indell county, North Carolina, June 16, 1805. When about two years old he came to Giles county, near Cornersville, Tennessee. He was converted to God when a youth in that same country while ploughing in the field of his father. The writer greatly regrets that, after repeated efforts to obtain the necessary *data* on which to write a full sketch of this good man's life and labors, he has not been successful. But he has determined to pen what he knows, believing that even this will be better than passing over in silence the life and labors of one who bore such an active part in the early work of the Church in Illinois. A letter from Dr. Beard, of Lebanon, says:

"My first knowledge of Rev. Cyrus Haynes was as a student of Cumberland College. When I reached that institution in May, 1830, he was there preparing for the ministry. A number of others whose names I call to mind were there engaged in the same way. Elam McCord, Silas N. Davis, F. C. Usher, J. D. Perryman, John Napier, T. B. Reynolds, were among the number. Mr. Haynes was one of the oldest of those whom I have mentioned. He continued a student to September of that year, when the vacation occurred. The next collegiate year commenced in November. Rev. Hiram McDaniel took charge of the farm and boarding house, and employed Bro. Haynes to superintend the farm. He spent one year in that business. In the following year he entered College again, and graduated in December of 1833. His class was one of the largest and best that ever left the institution. Among them were J. F. Ford and W. A. Scott. Both of these with Cyrus Haynes were licentiates when they graduated. Some time after his graduation he went to Illinois, and I only met him casually afterwards, mostly at meetings of the General Assembly. I have no knowledge of his earlier history. He was licensed and ordained, I suppose, by what was then Elk Presbytery, and is now a part of the same under the old name.

"I entertained a high opinion of Bro. Haynes, not so much on account of his ability as his integrity. I had unbounded confidence in the latter. He would have been considered rather eccentric. And he was inclined to extreme opinions; but he filled up my ideas of an honest man. I would have trusted him anywhere and to any extent, as far as integrity of purpose was concerned. From the commencement of my acquaintance with him he was more to me than a common friend and brother. The last time he was at my house he came late in the evening. The next morning I asked him to lead us in our family worship. He read an ordinary portion of Scripture, and commenced to lead us in singing the old hymn:

> "'Grace—'tis a charming sound,
> Harmonious to mine ear.'"

Before we were half through the hymn, however, he broke down under the force of his feelings, and wept like a child. It was a good morning service, and the last we ever held together in that capacity."

We find on the minutes of the Spring session of Vandalia Presbytery for 1834, that he was received as a licentiate from Princeton Presbytery, Kentucky. He was immediately placed by order of Presbytery on what was called the "Shelbyville circuit," on which he rode five months. From the records of this Presbytery we also find he was ordained to the whole work of the ministry at Bethany church, Shelby county, Illinois, on the 4th of October, 1834. Rev. John Barber, Jr., preached the ordination sermon from II. Cor. ii. 15, 16, and Rev. Joel Knight presided and gave the charge. At the same session we find an order for Mr. Haynes to ride "six weeks" the Shelbyville circuit; and near the close of the proceedings the record says he was dismissed by letter. He became a member of Sangamon Presbytery on the 6th of March, 1835, that body being in session at Mount Pleasant church, Morgan county. At this session Mr. Haynes was appointed principal commissioner to the General Assembly. He was also ordered to ride and preach in what was called "the military tract," and from this on for many years we find the records of this and other Presbyteries abounding with work connected with his name and influence. The following is from the pen of Rev. J. R. Lowrance:

"Mr. Haynes came to Morgan county, Ill., in 1836, and

labored in Sangamon Presbytery. He preached the funeral of a brother of mine—the first that ever occurred in my father's family. He traveled extensively in Central Illinois, and labored incessantly for several years. He opened a school in McDonough county, near Macomb. Just before this he was married to a Miss Smith, a most estimable and pious lady. This school was begun about 1837 or 1838. J. G. White and I were pupils in this school about 1839. He then removed his school to Cherry Grove. Here for several years he was quite successful in his school. W. S. Campbell, James McDowell, and others of useful lives were among his pupils. For some cause not remembered he quit this school, and about 1847 opened a school in Stouts Grove, McLean county, Illinois. Here his noble wife ended her useful life of toil, and the writer preached her funeral. After a few years of successful teaching he ceased to teach, entered on the active labors of a traveling minister, and went to the State of Iowa. Here he was again married to a Miss E. T. Biddle Dec. 3, 1852, another noble, intelligent, and pious lady. He traveled and preached for years all over Southern Iowa, an indefatigable worker. About 1860 his health gave way, and for a time his mind was somewhat injured. In 1869 or 1870 he removed to Northern Missouri, and there he sleeps in Jesus. He was a fine scholar and a great student. He published a very learned comment on the sixth chapter of Hebrews in or near 1840. A good reasoner, of great zeal and energy of character, he, as all others, had faults. But he loved his Church and his brethren. Above all, he loved his Savior, and was deeply devoted to the ministry."

We first met with Mr. Haynes at the General Assembly at Princeton in 1849. He was elected Clerk of that body, and it was the lot of the writer to be assigned to the same boarding place, room and bed with him. A very kind family of Episcopalians, whose name we have forgotten, entertained us very hospitably. For years afterwards, and until near his death, we often met in the Church judicatories, and often corresponded. He certainly was a man of more than ordinary energy, of untiring industry, and undeviating integrity. His efforts to afford the Church and the country better educational facilities than they had previously enjoyed were certainly very successful and worthy of all praise. The seminaries of Cherry Grove and Stouts Grove in that day were among the foremost institutions of learning in the State, and quite a number of men who are to-day in the front rank of society received their education, in whole or part, from these valuable schools.

The last time we met with Mr. Haynes was at the General Assembly in 1863 in the city of Alton. He was only a visitor, and evidently was laboring under some mental aberration. The war was then upon us. Darkness and uncertainty, like a universal pall, hung over the land. How much of his seeming mental infirmity might have resulted from brooding over this terrible national calamity, we do not know. We have never heard of any other probable cause. We do know that many strong minds and stout hearts quailed and sank down into the grave under that dreadful ordeal. He was with us in our family circle for some days after the Assembly closed, and, although it was evident that his mind was to some extent impaired, there was nothing in his acts which, in the slightest degree, could be construed into conduct immoral, or which cast any doubt upon the sincerity and uprightness of his former Christian or ministerial character. We felt relieved when we heard he had gone home,

> "Where the wicked cease from troubling,
> And *the weary are at rest.*"

Mr. Haynes left a devoted companion and several children, who are all respectable and respected wherever known.

Shortly after his second marriage he removed to Centreville, Iowa, where he remained until 1866, when he removed to Putnam county, Missouri. His health gradually declined, until July, 1871, he gave up all out-door life. He was confined to his room and much of the time to his bed until the 10th of December, when, in the language of his bereaved companion, feeling his end drawing near, he exclaimed, "I feel ready and willing to die;" and sinking into a peaceful slumber his soul was wafted to his Father's house on high.

### REV. JOHN BARBER, JR.

The following is furnished us by the brother of the deceased, Rev. W. W. M. Barber, of Windsor, Ill.:·

"Rev. John Barber, Jr., was born in Lincoln county, North Carolina, July 17, 1805, and immigrated with his father to Illinois in the year 1815, and settled with the family near Edwardsville, Madison county. He was converted at a Cumberland Presbyterian camp-meeting in Bond county, Illinois, at about the age of fifteen years, in what is now Bear Creek congregation, and soon became a member of the church. His conversion was very palpable and striking. Although he was so young and naturally very diffident, he passed through the congregation with expressions spontaneous, bold, clear and powerful, of his joy and happiness under a sense of the pardoning, saving mercy of God through Christ; and powerfully warning and exhorting others, and finally calling on inanimate nature—the trees and all—to witness that he then and there dedicated himself to the service of God. He was received as a candidate for the ministry by Illinois Presbytery at Shiloh, White county, Ill., October 10th, 1828, from Anderson Presbytery, he having first joined the latter while at college. There was an intermediate Presbytery appointed to license him, composed of John M. Berry, Thomas Campbell, Joel Knight, Gilbert Dodds, and John Barber, Sen.; but he, not having received his letter from the Anderson Presbytery, objected to being licensed when the intermediate Presbytery met, and it was not done till the regular session, which was held at Bear Creek, Montgomery county, Illinois, April 16th, 1829. He was ordained at the house of Joseph McAdams in Bond county, Illinois, March 12th, 1831, by Illinois Presbytery. By his own untiring efforts and what assistance his father could give him he became a respectable Greek scholar, having spent two years at old Princeton in Cumberland College. Soon after he left college he went into the active labors of the ministry, and was soon a spiritual, useful, and popular preacher. At about the age of twenty-five he was married to Miss E. A. Robinson, with whom he lived happily a little over eight years. A part of the time he suffered great bodily affliction, but enjoyed great peace of mind. He at length fell asleep in Jesus, leaving his companion with four children—three daughters and one son.

"Young John Barber, as he was called, was disposed to give himself entirely to the work of the ministry, but, the Church at that time not being able to do a great deal, and not being trained to do what she could, he, like other ministers, had to get a support from some other source. He became a school teacher, and soon became eminent in that calling, as well as in preaching. He possessed a clear, investigating, systematic mind. His discussions in preaching were thorough, clear, and logical, and with a ready flow of language. His reasonings and arguments were close, and his appeals almost resistless. But he was cut off in the midst of his usefulness. The Church had flattering prospects in him, and doubtless had the Church sustained him she might have enjoyed his labors much longer.

"While capable of active effort, in order to be as much devoted as possible to his ministerial calling, he became an agent in the Bible cause for a time, and again in the Tract cause as a colporteur. Under these circumstances he was strongly urged and temptations offered to him to change his ecclesiastical relations, and become connected with some other branch of the Church. It was urged that the Church to which he belonged did not appreciate his talents, usefulness, &c., or they would sustain him. He would be well sustained with others, and he would not be required to adopt any other system of theology to join the New School Presbyterians; and if he chose to join the Old School, why not? If he should have to adopt their Westminster Confession, he could make such mental reserves as were indispensable in order to meet his views and feelings in regard to doctrines. His father was also tempted in like manner as he was; but their loyalty to the Church was not measured by dollars and cents, and they therefore could not be bought. They had cast their lot with the Cumberland Presbyterian Church, and they would stand by her in her difficulties and trials, and co-operate with and assist others in bringing about reformations and improvements. They belonged to the Church. They had joined the army in good faith, and they never would desert it in order to support a family.

"His companion and four children are still living. The two oldest daughters and the son are married. The oldest is the wife of Rev. T. K. Hedges, who was a Cumberland Presbyterian minister, but is now of the Presbyterian Church. The second daughter married a farmer. All are religious and members of the Church, except the son, David F., who is a well-to-do farmer.

"John Barber, Jr., died April 22d, 1838, and was buried near Edwardsville, at what is called Ebenezer graveyard."

The action of Presbytery in regard to his death is found elsewhere. Mr. Barber died before our acquaintance in the State, but the universal verdict of the old citizens living who knew him is, that he was a man of more than ordinary talents and usefulness, and the entire people mourned his death.

### REV. ISAAC HILL.

Rev. J. W. Woods says:

"Rev. Isaac Hill was born the 22d day of December, 1784, and professed religion when he was thirty-six years of age in the State of Indiana, under the ministration of the first Cumberland Presbyterian ministers who crossed the Ohio river, and immediately joined the Church. He had a great desire to live thirty-six years more, that he might spend as much time in the service of God as he had spent in wandering away from him. He very soon began to be impressed with a sense of public duties, and accordingly began to exhort the people to seek salvation in Christ. He had to travel a long distance to meet the Kentucky Presbytery to become a candidate for the ministry. It was indeed with great difficulty and through some dangers that he made his way from Vigo county, Indiana, across the Ohio river when the waters were very high, to where the Presbytery convened. He was licensed to preach by Indiana Presbytery.

"He made a visit to the State of Illinois in September, 1826, and attended the first camp-meeting held in the eastern part of the State. He and Rev. John Knight, who also was a licentiate, were the only ministers present. It was then and there that a revival of religion commenced which diffused its blessings far and wide. Bro. Hill from that time visited that congregation statedly until he removed within its bounds in the Spring of 1828. None of our pioneer ministers were more earnest or zealous in the Master's work. He had a very strong and powerful voice, both in preaching and singing, and was eminently suited to camp-meeting work.

"He met Vandalia Presbytery at Mount Zion, Illinois, in June, 1833, at which time (June 15) he was ordained to the whole work of the ministry. Rev. Joel Knight preached the ordination sermon, Rev. John Barber, Jr., presided, and Rev. John Barber, Sen., gave the charge.

"Bro. Hill repeatedly traversed almost all the ground

which now comprises the Presbyteries of Foster and Hill, and parts of Vandalia and Decatur Presbyteries. He laid many foundations on which others have built, as his field of labor was so large. There was no resident minister of the Cumberland Presbyterian Church nearer than sixty miles in this State for at least eight years after he began to preach here; and the first within that bound was Rev. James Ashmore, who was converted and brought into the ministry in old Big Creek congregation where Bro. Hill resided and labored so faithfully until the weight of years and constant labor prostrated his manly form. It is not at all likely that so many ministers of the gospel have come out of any other congregation in the State as from the aforesaid congregation; and for his work's sake we think his memory is entitled to more consideration than any other minister whose field of labor has been within that of his. Emphatically he labored 'not for that meat which perisheth,' for the whole amount which he received during the time of his ministry would make but little if any more than a comfortable salary for one year at the present time. Large numbers of souls have been brought to the Savior by the work he has wrought for the gracious Master in his vineyard. Although his labors are ended, and nearly three decades have passed over the little mound which now marks the place where the toil-worn soldier's manly form now rests, he 'yet speaketh.' One of his eight sons, Rev. R. C. Hill, is now becoming old in the work of the ministry. Hill Presbytery was named in honor to his memory, and we trust it will become his most bright and enduring monument."

We regret that the above short letter from Bro. Woods is all we have been able to gather concerning this very useful pioneer minister, except that he was married to Margaret Cunningham April 16, 1807, and that he died February 11, 1853. We have been able to learn nothing of his family, save that Rev. R. C. Hill, of Loxa, Ill., is a worthy son of the deceased.

### REV. JOHN M. CAMERON.

I had almost despaired of obtaining any reliable account of this old father in Israel, and especially of the latter part of his life, when the following notice from the pen of B. B. Berry appeared in a recent number of the *Cumberland Presbyterian*, which we take great pleasure in transferring to our pages:

"Rev. John Miller Cameron was born in Elbert county, Georgia, on the twelfth day of August, 1791, and died at his residence after a painful and distressing affliction of two months' duration, on the twenty-first day of February, 1878, being eighty-six years, six months and nine days old.

"The deceased while a youth came with his father and family to Kentucky in the year 1804, and settled near the mouth of Green river, in Henderson county, at which place he was married to Mary Orendorff in the year 1811. From this place he removed to the Territory of Illinois, and settled in what is now White county, in the year 1813; removed from there to Belleville in St. Clair county in the year 1816; and from there to Sangamon county in the year 1818. This move was made about the time that Illinois was admitted into the Union. He stopped for a time near Springfield, after which he settled on Rock Creek in the same county, at which place the writer became intimately acquainted with him. He was at that time a candidate for the ministry in the bounds of Sangamon Presbytery, and about the year 1827 was licensed to preach. He devoted the principal part of his time to the ministry until 1832, when he removed to Fulton county, Illinois, where he was instrumental in building up several church organizations. He remained there until the year 1836, when he removed to the territory of Iowa, and settled for a time in Jefferson County, where he was an instrument in building up several more church organizations.

"Shortly after the admission of the State into the Union he again removed to Oskaloosa, Iowa, and at that place built up an organization and erected the first house of worship in the place. He devoted a portion of his time in visiting and preaching in the counties of Mahaska, Wapelo, Van Buren, Jefferson, Keokuk, Henry, Jasper, and others; was always punctual at the judicatures of the Church, and seldom failed to be at his own appointments.

"In the Spring of 1849 he started with his family across the plains, a distance of two thousand miles, to California. He arrived at a place now known as Fremont about the first of October of the same year; remained there but a short time; then went to Sacramento, where he remained during the Winter. In the Summer of 1850 he removed to Martinez, preaching occasionally until the Fall of 1851, when he removed to Sonoma county, near the present town of Sebastopol, where he purchased a farm on which he has ever since resided. He was set apart to the whole work of the ministry by the California Presbytery of the Cumberland Presbyterian Church in 1854. After this his time was mostly spent in visiting destitute places, preaching and organizing churches, and, after the organization, in visiting and supplying said churches until prevented by affliction and extreme old age. His wife died after a short illness at her home in Sonoma county, on the 25th day of March, 1876, at the advanced age of eighty-two years. Since this time the deceased seemed to be broken down in spirits, disconsolate, lonely, and dejected.

"Father Cameron was eminently a pioneer at the time of his settlement in Illinois in 1813, in Iowa in 1837, and in California in 1849. These States respectively had not been admitted into the Union. His life has been spent upon the frontier; and his occupation practically was to clear the way for those who would follow. He was a devoted husband, a kind and affectionate father, and a generous neighbor. He died as he had lived, faithful to every obligation. He was beloved by all who knew him; and a great many friends and relatives mourn their loss."

### REV. THOMAS CAMPBELL.

The subject of this notice was born in York District, South Carolina, October 31, 1786. While young he immigrated to Caldwell county, Kentucky. His parents were strict Presbyterians. He was married to Miss Elizabeth Robison March 22, 1810. He was first aroused to a sense of his lost condition under the preaching of Revs. Finis Ewing and William Barnett about the year 1815. He sought and found peace with God at his own home. His daughter, Mrs. Eliza J. Hughes, of Nilwood, Illinois, from whom we have received much that is herein written, says she has heard her father express himself about this event often, and he said: "It seemed as if all nature was changed to loveliness and praise: even the trees looked more beautiful than ever before." He soon felt it his duty to preach the gospel; and although he was married, and had a rising family, he placed himself under the care of the Anderson Presbytery, and was licensed by that Presbytery with Woods M. Hamilton and Gilbert Dodds.

He moved to Illinois in 1820 and settled temporarily in Pope county, having rented out his farm in Kentucky. He remained there only a year or two, and went back to Kentucky, where he stayed but a short time. Then he sold out and removed in 1823 to Sangamon county, Illinois, where he spent the remainder of his life. His home was on what was called "Little Spring Creek." He bought an improvement and entered the land at the first land sales ever opened in Springfield.

We find he presented a letter of dismission and recommendation from Anderson Presbytery to Illinois Presbytery as a licentiate October 5, 1824, and was received. This session of Presbytery was held at old Hopewell church, in White county. He was ordained to the whole work of the ministry at Bear Creek church, Montgomery county, in April, 1825. Rev. D. W. McLin preached the ordination sermon, presiding and giving the charge also.

Like most of the ministers of his day, his opportunities were limited to procure an education, and, the country being new, he had to make his own living on his farm. But he was very industrious and studious, and passed a creditable examination on the English sciences required by the Book of Discipline. In looking over the records of his Presbytery we find him usually present at her meetings, and always taking an active part in her proceedings. He studied the Scriptures. They were emphatically the source from whence he derived most of his information. He was provided, however, with the commentaries both of Clark and Henry. He preached without manuscript: did not use even notes, and always held up Jesus and his cross in every sermon. He was greatly useful, and much beloved by those who knew him. He traveled far and near across the wild prairies to carry the news of salvation to the people, who always heard him gladly. His own house in Sangamon county was a preaching place and a place for Sunday-school. A Sunday-school was organized in his house, with David S. Taylor as superintendent. He and his wife first united with a little society four miles from his home at the house of Abraham Duff, where Mr. Campbell preached for several years. He aided in building up a number of congregations in that and adjoining counties. Of course, when Sangamon Presbytery was stricken off from Illinois Presbytery he was included in the membership of Sangamon.

Mr. Campbell was the father of thirteen children, five of whom are gone to their final home. He was very strict in the observance of the Sabbath; was a strong temperance man—joined the "American Temperance Society" long before the "Washingtonians" or any other temperance society was known. Says our informant: "He believed in the life and power of religion, preached repentance to sinners and perseverance to Christians, preached in the power and demonstration of the Spirit, and usually got hold of the feelings of the people." The same party relates this incident: "Once, when he was preaching at a camp-meeting at Rock Creek, while speaking of the sinner's lost condition, he related a circumstance that happened when he was living in Pope county of a little girl who was lost and never found. A stranger in the audience was so wrought upon that he cried out with alarm at the top of his voice."

His death was very sudden and unexpected. It occurred on the 11th of May, 1850. His disease was something like cholera, although there was not thought to be any in the country that year. He felt a little unwell in the morning, but ate his breakfast as usual and went out in the field to plant corn. His son saw him fall on his face. He was carried or hauled to the house, a doctor sent for, but before his arrival he was dying, and soon after expired. There was no minister near enough to attend the funeral, but a large concourse of citizens and neighbors followed him to the grave. At the time of his death he was a member of Harris Presbytery, (which only existed a year or two, being a part of Sangamon Presbytery, it was re-attached,) which, at its session in October following, adopted an appropriate minute respecting the death of Mr. Campbell. He was buried in what is called the "Morgan grave yard." Some years later his companion, a very worthy Christian woman, was laid by his side. His grave has a neat but plain tomb-stone, with his name, birth, death and calling, and then this sentence: "Precious in the sight of the Lord is the death of his saints." The death of Mr. Campbell occurred before our acquaintance in the State, but we have found plentiful evidences of his activity and great usefulness all over the interior counties.

### REV. NICHOLAS CARPER.

One of the earliest ministers of Vandalia Presbytery, and one greatly beloved, was Rev. Nicholas Carper, a colored preacher. Of his early life but little is known to the writer. We find the following reference to his life and early ministry by Judge Ewing in his "Historical Memoirs," which, perhaps, gives the true account of his origin: "The session of 1836 was held at the Bethel church in Boon county. Among the members of this Synod appears the name of Rev. Nicholas Caoper," (evidently a misprint for Carper,) "a colored man of rare endowments as a public speaker. He was a bright mulatto, having a very fine face, and being of large, portly person. I have heard him preach from the same stand at a camp-meeting with Ewing, Morrow, Sloan, and others of the old preachers. I noticed that he was appointed on a committee with S. C. Davis and John M. Foster to examine the minutes of the Barnett Presbytery. He had formerly been a slave, and was the property of William Jack, of Lexington. He obtained his freedom, and became a minister in the St. Louis Presbytery—at least, he appeared from that Presbytery in Synod. I think I never heard a speaker with so fine a voice. It was strong, yet smooth, melodious and musical. When raised to a high key it was like a bugle note from a silver trumpet."—Page 15.

We find his name at an early day on the roll of ministers of Vandalia Presbytery. In the records of the Spring session of 1839 we find Mr. Carper joined by letter, and from other reliable sources we learn that he was then living in the American bottom opposite St. Louis, where he remained until his death. Some where near the little village of Brooklyn, between Venice and East St. Louis, was the place of his residence. The writer never met him, but in St. Louis Presbytery, and Vandalia, also, the older brethren speak of him in the highest terms as a man of extraordinary powers of mind and ability as a speaker. Nor were his abilities of mind and powers of speech more noteworthy than his humility and devout piety.

The following is from Rev. James B. Braly, of Steelville, Mo., who knew Mr. Carper well: "Bro. Carper's education was limited, but still his language was usually chaste, and frequently elegant. He was not a systematic preacher. When he divided his subject he seldom paid any attention to his divisions, sometimes treating the last division first. He was truly eloquent. His gestures were natural and graceful. His voice was shrill but very musical—I think the most musical voice I ever heard. His singing was full of melody. He could always secure the attention of his audience. His preaching was usually very effective. He brought his whole soul into his subject, and his applications were powerful. He was truly a wonderful man. He did not have a great variety. Often he preached from the same text, and would frequently make mistakes, confounding Bible names. But his mistakes were not usually noticed by his hearers, they being carried away by his eloquence. You may think, my brother, that I have overdrawn the picture, he being a man of color; but if you could have seen and heard him, I think you would agree with me that he was a wonderful man." Mr. Braly gives the following incident of Mr. Carper: "He preached occasionally from a text he called the 'Devil's text:' 'Ye shall not surely die.' At a camp-meeting held by the Methodists, I think in St. Louis county, he was invited to preach. It was not long after he came into our bounds. In his preface he told his hearers that there was an old preacher amongst them who had traveled and preached very extensively. He went on to describe him, and said he had done much mischief. There was an old preacher by the name of Heath who lived in St. Louis and had traveled very extensively, and while Carper was talking the preachers all began to whisper and wonder if it was not Heath. But the old man told them after a while that he meant the Devil."

The following letter from Rev. J. M. Bone, for many years a minister in Vandalia Presbytery, will be of additional interest. Mr. Bone now resides at Pomona, Kansas:

"I met Bro. Carper but a few times. Though he was a member of Vandalia Presbytery, yet he never attended any of its sessions. He moved from St. Louis and settled in the American bottom, a few miles above East St. Louis, and soon after he settled there he sent his letter and was received as a member of Vandalia Presbytery. At that time he was preaching to a congregation of colored people in St. Louis, either Congregationalists or New School Presbyterians, I don't know which, and continued to preach to them some time after he settled in Illinois. Congregationalists, Baptists and Presbyterians frequently invited him to assist them in protracted meetings. They loved to have him. He was a good revivalist.

"I met him at a camp-meeting at Beaver Creek, in the south part of Bond county, Illinois, and there I learned from him all I know of his history. He was born a slave. His father was one-fourth French. He was married before he professed religion. He said in a discourse at the camp-meeting, that when he was fourteen years old he knew nothing but to lie with his toes in the ashes and run at the call of his master. He had no knowledge of books or their design. When he decided that it was his duty to preach the gospel he devoted himself to the work of preparing for the ministry; and when he was ordained he stood an examination on all the parts of trial required by our Book. He was licensed and ordained by the Lexington Presbytery. He devoted all his time to the work of the ministry. In the meantime he bought and paid for himself, wife and two daughters. Two sons were sold as slaves and taken South. He never saw or heard from them after. He was a large, portly, good-looking mulatto man. He weighed about two hundred pounds, and when I saw him I suppose he was about sixty years old.

"Bro. Carper was a good, acceptable preacher. He used good language. His manner was solemn. He presented his thoughts clearly and some times impressively. His preaching was mostly experimental and practical. He was powerful in exhortation. He knew his place in the society of white people. He was modest and retiring, and never intruded himself so as to give offense. But in the pulpit he was at home. There he spoke his mind boldly and independently. He reproved sin sharply, and urged the service of God in Christ tenderly and in love. He died, I think, in the American bottom, but I know nothing of the particulars of his death."

The brief notice of his death by Vandalia Presbytery may be found elsewhere.

### REV. JAMES M'DOWELL.

The following is furnished us by his son, Joseph W. McDowell, now residing near Hopedale, Illinois, and is copied mainly from a sketch prepared by his (Mackinaw) Presbytery, and published in the *Cumberland Presbyterian* April 17, 1849:

Mr. McDowell departed this life on October 22d, 1846, in the forty-eighth year of his age. He was born in North Carolina of pious parents, who removed to Robison county, Tennessee, prior to the revival of 1800. His father was an elder in the Presbyterian Church, and took his stand with the revival party. The subject of our notice embraced religion on the 2d of August, 1822. He was received as a candidate for the ministry by Logan Presbytery in the Fall of 1823. He was licensed by the same Presbytery in October of 1825, and immediately started on what was called the Green River circuit. From this to April, 1830, his time was mostly spent in riding the circuit and preaching. At the session of Presbytery in April, 1830, he was ordained. From his journal kept during this time we find him a laborious and very successful minister of Christ. As a sample of the work done and privations endured by our first ministers, we give this from his journal, the first six month's labor after his licensure, from October, 1825, to April, 1826. He says: "Since last Presbytery forty-seven made profession of religion; twelve joined the Church. I have received $9.25 in cash, four vests, three pairs of socks, one pair of pantaloons, and two cravats. My expenses were $5.75." It will be seen that his pay in money was just $3.50. Again he records: "From April 20th to November 12th I rode one thousand, seven hundred and thirty-eight miles; preached one hundred and sixty-one times; fifty-four professed religion over and above the number who professed at camp-meetings. I received by way of remuneration $27.25; my expenses, $3.62." This is a fair sample of after years.

In September, 1830, he was married, and removed immediately to Tazewell county, Illinois. At that time there was but one ordained minister in the present bounds of Mackinaw Presbytery, and but one organized church, and this one embraced an area about fifty miles in diameter. Mr. McDowell entered at once with great zeal and faithfulness into the work of preaching Christ in this vast and important field. His health failed, however, some years before his death, so that he preached but seldom; yet he continued greatly useful to the Church. He was a sound and safe counsellor in the judicatures of the Church, and of great help to candidates for the ministry. At one time he took a young man, a Bro. Hutchison, to his house, and kept him under his tuition till he was able to stand a creditable examination on all parts of trial preparatory to ordination. This young man afterwards died in the triumphs of faith, having preached with much acceptance and success for several years.

The preaching of Mr. McDowell was about equally divided between theology, experience and practice. He was not what the world called a great preacher, but was a man "full of faith and of the Holy Ghost." He is said to have been rather reserved in conversation when not well acquainted, but those who knew him best loved him most. His last illness was long and very severe, but he bore it with great patience and fortitude, and departed without doubt or fear in full assurance of eternal life through that Jesus he had so long and faithfully preached. He was a humble, unostentatious man, having no jealous spirit, and always rejoicing in the honor bestowed upon, and the success accomplished by, his ministering brethren. He did much to plant the standard of the cross and of the Cumberland Presbyterian Church in Mackinaw Presbytery. Many are the reminiscences now all over that country connected with his name and labors.

www.ingramcontent.com/pod-product-compliance
Lightning Source LLC
Chambersburg PA
CBHW031828230426
43669CB00009B/1272